RE

FROM

THE REGION'S

FAVORITE

RESTAURANTS

Vegetarian

Southwest

LON WALTERS

PHOTOGRAPHS BY
CHRISTOPHER MARCHETTI

NORTHLAND PUBLISHING

To my mother, Helen, who insisted cooking was as much a man's task

as anyone else's in the family; and to my life partner, Margi, who convinced

me there is as much fun in preparation as in dining.

Text © 1998 by Lon Walters
Photographs © 1998 by Northland Publishing
All rights reserved.

www.northlandbooks.com

Composed in the United States of America
Manufactured in China

All temperatures in this cookbook refer to the Fahrenheit scale.
The use of trade names does not imply an endorsement by the product manufacturer.

FIRST IMPRESSION
ISBN 10: 0-87358-710-3
ISBN 13: 978-0-87358-710-5

Library of Congress Catalog Card Number 98-11513
Walters, Lon.
    Vegetarian Southwest : recipes from the region's favorite
restaurants / Lon Walters ; photographs by Christopher Marchetti.
        p.   cm.
    Includes bibliographical references and index.
    ISBN 0-87358-710-3
    1. Vegetarian cookery. 2. Cookery, American   Southwestern style.
I. Title.
TX837.W275 1998
641.5'636'0979—dc21   98-11513

CONTENTS

ACKNOWLEDGMENTS

As creators of these recipes, contributing chefs strived to combine ingredients to ensure they met their high standards for flavor and presentation. All willingly gave their time, and a few kitchen secrets, so you could enjoy a new level of vegetarian cooking. They are the reason for this book.

My testers realized that cooking is much like any art: it is difficult to duplicate the results with every stroke of the brush. A stove may be a little warmer, the chili pepper a little fresher and the spices a bit stronger each time it is prepared. So results varied. They pursued the intent of each chef to ensure the magic of the recipe was never lost.

Thank you to Rebecca Tarnow who remarkably kept her enthusiasm throughout every trial, John and Barbara Wade who zealously tackled every recipe presented, and to the staff of Northland Publishing. At the eleventh hour, they took on more recipes to ensure all were good, and fun, for the fledgling cook.

Also a special thanks to Chio Black who provided much of the historical perspective on Native American influence in Southwestern dishes. To my wife Margi for her patience, pushing and proofing. It was she who proved to me anything is possible. And to my mother, who planted the seed on what a joy cooking can be.

The delight in cooking one of these recipes is not necessarily in the end product, but in the endless options available in preparation and flavoring of a dish. The pleasure of hitting on a delicious combination is a sense of satisfaction you will not soon forget. These folks who contributed helped me keep this in perspective.

The publisher wishes to thank recipe testers Jim Linde and Chris Dane for extra and much appreciated help; Judy Walker and the staff of *The Arizona Republic* for the use of their kitchen studio; food stylist Cathy Marshall and photographer Christopher Marchetti for their creative abilities and their long hours; and the following Flagstaff stores for the generous loan of props: Pier 1 imports, Dillard's Department Store, Warner's Nursery and Landscape Company, and The Kitchen Source.

INTRODUCTION

D efining Southwestern cuisine is a problem for many food writers. First, the territory called "Southwest" is as much in debate as are the regional foods. The land covers thousands of square miles and is generally agreed upon to include all of Arizona and New Mexico. From there it is anyone's guess.

However, the remaining high plains area usually includes southern Utah, the southwest corner of Colorado, and a far western piece of Texas. I believe this to be far more traditional than other definitions that include southern California and Oklahoma.

Second, there is considerable confusion about what constitutes a Southwestern dish. The real history of Southwestern cooking is so muddled it is difficult to sort out just what can be called "original."

During the early 1980s the basis for most Southwestern creations was Tex-Mex. Texas and Mexico represented the strongest influences on an emerging cuisine, and it was simple to justify any dish with a Tex-Mex bias as authentic. However, within a few years many innovative chefs took hold of Southwestern recipes and standards came tumbling down. Dining at a restaurant with a menu affirmed to be Southwestern could have included such unlikely combinations as duck carnitas, shrimp chili, and avocado enchiladas. Although most of it was delicious, it was also so diverse that one could not know what to expect in a Southwestern restaurant.

I always thought of Southwestern food as having a strong Mexican and Native American influence, a blend of indigenous foods with Spanish stylization. But this is not always the case. Throwing a bit of chili powder into a pot of beans does not a Southwestern meal make.

The basis for much of the early Southwestern foods was corn. It was prolific and a Native American staple for centuries before Europeans came on the scene. Most modern recipes that use cornmeal came from the original inhabitants of the Old West. For example, corn tortillas, commonly thought of as a Mexican innovation, were really developed by Native Americans as a brittle corn bread called *piki*.

What can be conceded is that Southwestern cuisine is highly regional. A Southwestern restaurant in Texas will serve decidedly different cuisine from one found in New Mexico.

Southwestern cuisine is also remarkable in that many I'll-never-give-up-my-meat diners never know the difference if a dish is made with chicken, duck, shrimp, or no meat at all. Creative chefs have accomplished amazing things with these, and other, very basic ingredients.

So with a wildly free hand, I assembled this anthology of vegetarian dishes with a Southwestern flair. Some dishes are healthier than others, but all are vegetarian.

To gather a variety unlike any printed before, I contacted restaurants in Colorado, New Mexico, and Arizona. Many are from nationally recognized chefs, and there is also a fair representation from locally popular restaurants. Each is astounding—but each in a different way.

These recipes vary widely in complexity. Some are challenging and designed for those who enjoy the preparation at least as much as the consumption. Others are easier. To help fledgling cooks, some recipes include simpler substitutions. While this may reduce the quality of the dish, it will get to the table much faster.

Most ingredients are available at your neighborhood grocery store. A few recipes may require spices from a Latino market or by special order. Remember, one of the joys of the recipes in this book is found in trying new flavorings and combinations. If you don't understand an ingredient or instruction in a recipe, turn to the glossary on page 159. If you scan this "dictionary" before beginning, much of the mystery surrounding Southwestern cooking will be dispelled.

Don't be timid about preparing what at first glance appears to be a complex recipe. All have been tested by folks who neither live in the kitchen nor work at culinary schools. They were assembled by cooks who enjoy making a meal and were thrilled to find new tastes and techniques. While some recipes require a few more preparation steps than a simple vegetable casserole, none of the steps are too difficult for the home kitchen. If you still feel it necessary to gather your sea legs into Southwestern cooking before embarking on a long recipe, try making a dish with only a few ingredients. Then, with the confidence of a sea captain, you can thoroughly enjoy the exploration into the remarkable combinations presented in this book.

Cooking is an expression of your tastes, and no two dishes are ever assembled, or taste, exactly alike, even when made from the same recipe. Just a smidgen of extra salt or a few more slices of onion will change the flavor of a recipe. This is what makes food preparation so remarkable, and so personal. I suggest making the dish as listed the first time around; then let your creative juices roll, adding and deleting as you like the next time you make the dish. "Author's notes" at the end of the recipes include time-saving tips, simple substitutions, and other relevant commentary. These are merely suggestions, and your first choice should always be to follow the chef's intentions.

Vegetarian Southwest is intended to supplement an emerging vegetarian lifestyle choice with recipes from restaurants you love as well as from places you've never heard of. It was a joy to discuss regional vegetarian cooking and preparation with this talented group of chefs. I hope you enjoy the many creative selections.

CHILES

CHILES ARE SUCH an integral part of Southwestern dining, few residents hesitate to use them anymore. The rest of the world may someday stand up and applaud the culinary potential of chiles, but for now the Southwestern United States and Mexico rule their use. Believed to have originated in the western hemisphere, varieties spread worldwide to become an essential part of many European and Asian dishes, but not as extensively as in the Southwest and Mexico.

Unfortunately, many who have had the hapless experience of tasting a chile pepper with a heat just this side of a forest fire have never returned. They have missed dozens of mild and flavor-filled varieties that enhance delectable dishes.

A major problem chiles may suffer is consumer bewilderment. Called chile "peppers," they are not related to black pepper. As a fresh item, they are vegetables; as a dried item, they are a spice. Botanically, they are berries; horticulturally, they are fruits. Is it spelled chile, chili, or chilli? No wonder people are confused and balk at experimenting.

Exacerbating the problem is confusion about just what a chile is. Different regions of the United States and Mexico call the varieties by different names. A poblano is also called a pasilla, and red Fresno chiles are sometimes labeled red jalapeños. And look out, taste buds, if you confuse the look-alike Anaheim and New Mexico green chiles. The first is mild, but the latter makes an excellent statement in the heat department.

Blame none other than Christopher Columbus for the start of all this confusion. Besides his navigational errors, he thought the hot taste of chiles he "discovered" was really that of a black pepper. The word has stuck ever since.

The word "chile" is a Spanish adulteration of an Aztec name for the pepper plant. Chiles were one of the earliest plants cultivated and have been found in Peruvian burial sites dating from 6200 B.C. They were extremely popular with Mayans, Aztecs, and Incas. Stateside, Native Americans gathered wild chiles in the Sonoran Desert and used them as a spice and trading material with other tribes.

By the mid-sixteenth century, chile plants reached into Europe and Asia and today are grown around the world. Chile plants cross-pollinate easily so there are many hybrids. New Mexico is the largest U.S. producer, followed by California, Texas, and Arizona.

The chile's famous heat comes from a powerful compound called "capsaicin." Capsaicin survives freezing and cooking to retain its fiery taste. The amount of capsaicin in a chile decides its heat factor. Some very mild chiles, like the Anaheim, contain smaller traces compared to the challenging habanero.

If a renegade chile tingles your palate beyond a reasonable comfort level, drink some milk to salvage your taste buds. Starchy foods work, too, like bread or rice. Alcoholic beverages are not a viable option—they actually increase a chile's heat by ensuring faster absorption of capsaicin.

Today chiles are commonly available canned, powdered, dried, and fresh. In major market areas they are also sold frozen. My personal bias is to avoid canned chiles except as a condiment. As a topping for a sandwich or diced for an accent, they work. However, as a major part of an entrée, like chiles rellenos, they are lifeless.

On the other hand, powdered chiles are excellent for waking up flavors. As an addition to sauces and as a seasoning, they are wonderful. Next time you're shopping near a Latino market, pick up a few jars. Look for a deep, rich color to ensure their valuable chile oil is still present for the best flavor. If possible, rub a sample between your fingers: The aroma should tell all.

Dried chiles are best for sauces. They reconstitute well and taste remarkably similar to fresh. However, due to the drying process, they do carry more punch—ounce for ounce at least twice that of fresh. Dried chiles should have a little flex if they are freshly dried and should be rich, and consistent, in color, as well as whole and unbroken. Crushed and torn chiles will have a diluted flavor.

Fresh chiles are superb and maximize a pot of chili's potential. As a general guide to purchasing fresh chiles, the smaller the chile, the hotter. But even smaller chiles can be toned down by removal of the seeds and veins or by simply using fewer in a recipe. Also, the redder (or riper) the chile, the sweeter the flavor.

When selecting fresh, just think in terms of other items you normally select on produce shelves. Look for bright, nicely shaped, and firm chiles. Also, make sure that the right chile is in the grocery bin. They are often mixed, so do not hesitate to talk to a produce clerk. Fresh chiles should be washed, dried, wrapped in paper towels, and stored in the refrigerator. Plastic bags are not user-friendly to any chiles and accelerate spoiling.

Some cooks are very sensitive to capsaicin. Use protective rubber gloves while seeding and deveining. It may sound like overkill, but your skin will thank you. Never, never touch your face or eyes while cleaning chiles. You'll do this only once to learn an uncomfortable lesson.

Each chile has a distinctive flavor and aroma. Lucky Southwestern residents can choose from among a broad variety for their favorite recipes. Mind you, this doesn't make selection any easier. Hundreds of accessible varieties present an over-whelming "trial-by-fire" opportunity, especially since many Southwesterners were raised without learning how to select, prepare, and cook chiles.

The chile pepper's reputation as a food only for those with an iron palate is undeserved. While there are varieties that would check out as reasonable substitutes for rocket fuel, there are also many mild, sweet, flavorful chiles. Here is a primer in "chileology."

Anaheim Usually green but red are also sold in larger markets. Closely related to the New Mexican chile. Anaheims are mild on the chile scale; most anyone can eat them. They are long (about six inches) and tapered. Available year-round, they are superb for rellenos. Anaheims are also wonderful roasted and are used to perk up other dishes.

Ancho Common in Latino markets, anchos are dried poblanos. They look like ugly, large raisins (ancho in Spanish means "wide"). Sometimes mistaken for another popular dried chile—the pasilla—anchos are sweet and mild and used in many sauces. By far the most popular dried chile, it is available fresh year-round and as a powder.

Cayenne Certainly one of the most popular chiles in powder form, cayenne is valuable in many sauces and soups. Often thought of as the hottest of the hot, it doesn't hold a candle to real chile monsters like the habanero. But don't be misled: It does make a state-ment. Tart and pungent, it is an excellent spice.

Chipotle   Another dried chile, actually a dried and smoked jalapeño. Near the middle in the heat department, it tastes smoky and sweet. Chipotles are two to three inches long and look like wide, elongated prunes. Widely used in Southwestern dishes, including sauces, soups, and salsa.

Habanero Crowned the king of heat, habaneros come in many colors, including green, yellow, and red. Most are approximately two inches long and almost that wide. They are many, many times hotter than cayennes or jalapeños, so be careful cleaning, cutting, and eating. Habanero's oils are very strong and can easily irritate skin. Despite its reputation as a "barn burner," habaneros taste fruit-like and are a delicious addition to many dishes.

Jalapeño Where would nachos be without jalapeños? It was named the state pepper of Texas and is one of the most popular chiles in the world. Found in both green and red forms, both have about the same heat content. Jalapeños are two to three inches in length, tapered, and very similar to serranos in flavor.

New Mexican   Look much like Anaheims but a bit wider. Flavor is like a hot green bell pepper. Found as New Mexican red and New Mexican green, both are about in the middle of the heat scale. Very good roasted and excellent in soups, sauces, and chutneys.

Pasilla A dried chile, long in shape and black in color. Also called chile negro, it is used in many sauces and as a spice in powdered form. Often confused with a fresh or dried poblano. A very popular chile in Mexico.

Piquin Also spelled "pequin." Small (about one-half inch), orange-red in color, and very hot. Often dried and ground as a spice, will perk up almost any dish. Sweet, smoky flavor. Cayenne fans use piquins for a change of pace.

Poblano A very popular chile due to its wonderfully mild flavor; about as hot as an Anaheim. Rarely eaten raw, poblanos are usually roasted and cooked in stews, sauces, and many other dishes. Measures four to five inches and is deep, rich green or dark red in appearance. Green poblanos are often used in stuffed-chile dishes.

Serrano A hot chile used in sauces or as an accent. Small—only about an inch or so in length—it does pack a punch. Green or red varieties are both commonly roasted to bring out flavor. Sometimes substituted for jalapeño. Caution is advised due to the biting heat.

Yellow Hot Wax Also called Güero or banana chile, it is yellow and waxy in texture. Can be as long as five inches but is usually a three-to-four-inch tapered chile. In the middle of the heat range and used primarily to make yellow mole sauces or for pickling. Also used in salads and sauces.

ROASTING CHILES

ROASTING CHILES is the most popular preparation before inclusion in a dish. The rich, smoky flavor is delicious. Roasting is not a mystery and can be done in any kitchen. Roast over an open flame, in a broiler, or over a grill. Whichever method you use, start with a chile that is firm and fresh. Here's a foolproof way to amaze your friends.

1. Wash, dry, and arrange all chiles on a broiler or grill rack.

2. Place rack about 1 inch above a medium-hot grill or under a preheated broiler, or hold it about 1 inch above the flame of a gas stove.

3. Turn chiles frequently until blistered and lightly browned (not charred) all over.

4. Remove and place chiles in a bowl and cover with plastic wrap or place them in a plastic or paper bag. As chiles steam, or "sweat," their skins will loosen.

5. After sweating the chiles, remove unwashed chile skins (washing at this point will remove the flavor of the natural oils), then remove seeds and ribs (wear plastic gloves until you determine whether your hands can tolerate the oils).

Soups

$\mathcal{S}$oups have been a part of Southwestern cuisine for centuries, beginning with broths created by Native Americans from indigenous vegetables. Centuries ago, soups were a main meal among peasants and were served to royalty as precursors to more outrageous entrées. For the peasants, soups were a means of creatively stretching limited resources; for royalty, they were another opportunity for the court chef to formulate provocative samples of his expertise. An endless variety of hot and cold soups was developed. Today a bowl of soup is appreciated as a culinary delight at lunch or dinner.

Soups are far more filling and hearty than most beverages, and a lot more exciting to fix, so canned, packaged, and fresh soups are gaining a new level of respect, actually coming full circle. Unlike other dishes, there are few rules for soups. It is possible to mix and cook almost anything in hot water. For creating your own Southwestern variety, the following should steer you in the right direction.

> Don't get excited about timing. It's done when it's done and will usually last well beyond that. Serving underdone soup is not a sin either.

> Don't overseason. Let the natural ingredients bring out the quality. The temptation is to season to taste during preparation, but cooking dramatically expands the flavoring potential of seasonings and even mild seasonings can become overpowering. Better to season after, or lightly during, rather than before preparation. Salt and pepper are typically the worst offenders.

> No special equipment is needed to prepare a delightful soup. Don't get caught up in having just the right pot or stirring implement.

> Soups are great when made ahead and will freeze well. The exceptions are those made with cream and cheeses.

The creations these chefs formulated are simply delicious. However, if you find seasonings in the following soup recipes overwhelming, change them. Although they vary in complexity, each is a treasure representing the best the Southwest has to offer.

Caldo de Queso

Cafe Poca Cosa, Tucson, Arizona

CHEF SUZANNA DAVILLA

¼ cup vegetable oil

4 large potatoes, unpeeled and cut into large chunks

1 large yellow onion, cut into wedges

3 scallions, finely chopped

2 cloves garlic, roasted

6 Anaheim green chiles, roasted, peeled, seeded,
  and cut into strips

1½ tablespoons dried oregano

1 quart vegetable stock (about 2½ 13¾-ounce cans)

5 large tomatoes, roasted and chopped in blender

1 quart whole milk

2½ pounds Monterey jack cheese, shredded

Salt and pepper to taste

Cilantro for garnish

Add oil to a large soup pot and heat until medium hot. Add potatoes and cook until lightly golden. Sauté yellow onion and two-thirds of the chopped scallions with the potatoes. Add garlic, green chiles, and oregano. Drain excess oil. Add vegetable stock and bring to a boil. Lightly stir in tomatoes and slowly add milk. Lower heat to a simmer and add 2 pounds of the Monterey jack cheese. Stir until cheese melts. Add salt and pepper to taste.

Top each serving with remaining cheese and scallions and garnish with cilantro.

SERVES 6

AUTHOR'S NOTE: The cheese is heavy in this dish, so be sure to stir it frequently over low heat in order to prevent the cheese from burning on the bottom of the pan.

Roasted Eggplant and Tomato Soup

Enchantment Resort, Sedona, Arizona

CHEF CHAD LUETHJE

1 eggplant, sliced

2½ pounds tomatoes, diced

½ yellow onion, peeled and quartered

1 red bell pepper, sliced

Olive oil to coat vegetables

1½ quarts vegetable stock (about 3½ 13¾-ounce cans)

2 garlic cloves, minced

1 sprig fresh basil, chopped (or ½ teaspoon dried)

1 sprig fresh oregano, chopped (or ½ teaspoon dried)

1 sprig fresh thyme, chopped (or ½ teaspoon dried)

Salt to taste

Cayenne to taste

1 teaspoon lemon juice

Preheat oven to 350 degrees.

Coat vegetables with olive oil and roast until skins have split and the vegetables are starting to brown nicely. In a large pot, combine vegetables, stock, garlic, herbs, seasonings, and lemon juice. Reduce to one-third by boiling, uncovered, for approximately 20 to 30 minutes. Purée and strain. Adjust seasonings and serve.

SERVES 6

AUTHOR'S NOTE: If fresh herbs are not available, substitute ½ teaspoon dried.

Carrot-Ginger Soup

The Heartline Café, Sedona, Arizona

CHEF CHARLES A. CLINE

¼ cup vegetable oil

1 tablespoon chopped garlic

1½ tablespoons peeled, and chopped ginger

2 leeks, diced into 1- to 2-inch pieces

3 ribs celery, diced into 1- to 2-inch pieces

2 yellow or white onions, diced into 1- to 2-inch pieces

10 to 12 carrots, diced into 1- to 2-inch pieces

2 quarts (8 cups) water

Salt and pepper to taste

I n a heavy-bottomed pot, heat the oil and sauté garlic and ginger until aromatic, but do not brown. Add leeks, celery, and onions and cook until tender. Add carrots and water. Simmer until carrots are soft. Purée in blender or food processor. Adjust seasoning to taste.

SERVES 6 TO 8

AUTHOR'S NOTE: This is a very mild soup. For a slightly stronger flavor, Chef Cline suggests substituting pure coconut milk (14-ounce can) for an equal portion of water and adding curry powder (1 tablespoon).

Roasted Poblano Chile Soup

Top of Sedona, Sedona, Arizona

CHEF COREY ERWIN

6 whole poblano chiles

¼ cup vegetable oil, plus some for coating chiles

6 stalks celery, diced

1 medium onion, chopped

1 tablespoon chopped garlic

1 green bell pepper, seeded and diced

1 red bell pepper, seeded and diced

1 bunch scallions, diced

2 yellow squash, diced

1 bunch fresh cilantro, chopped

2 carrots, peeled and diced

3 bay leaves

1½ teaspoons cumin

1 quart vegetable stock (about 2½ 13¾-ounce cans)

Salt to taste

Cilantro for garnish

Crushed tortilla chips for garnish

Preheat oven to 400 degrees. Coat the poblano chiles with a light coating of vegetable oil and roast on a cookie sheet for 20 minutes. Remove from oven, place in a stainless steel or glass bowl, and cover tightly with plastic wrap. Allow them to cool for about 20 minutes. Peel and seed the chiles and coarsely chop them.

In a large, heavy pot, heat the oil on medium heat until hot. Add the celery, onion, garlic, green and red bell peppers, scallions, squash, cilantro, and carrots, and sauté until vegetables are translucent, about 10 to 12 minutes, stirring constantly. Add the bay leaves, cumin, and vegetable stock and bring to a boil. Simmer for 5 minutes. Add salt to taste, if desired.

Garnish with chopped cilantro and crushed tortilla chips.

SERVES 6

~~~~~~~~~~

Butternut Squash Bisque with Cinnamon Maple Cream

The Tack Room, Tucson, Arizona

CHEF RODNEY TIMM

BUTTERNUT SQUASH BISQUE

- 1 medium onion, chopped
- ½ large leek, white part only, chopped
- 2 tablespoons olive oil
- 5 pounds butternut squash, peeled, seeds removed, and cut into chunks
- ¾ gallon vegetable stock (about seven 13¾-ounce cans) or water
- 2 ancho chiles, seeded and torn into large pieces
- ½ cup honey, preferably mesquite
- 2 tablespoons chopped fresh sage (or 2 teaspoons dried)
- 2 tablespoons chopped fresh thyme (or 2 teaspoons dried)

Salt and pepper to taste

Cinnamon Maple Cream (recipe follows)

Chopped cilantro for garnish

In a large stock pot, sauté onion and leek in oil until lightly brown. Add squash and vegetable stock and simmer for about 1 hour or until squash is tender. Toast ancho chiles in a hot skillet, pressing down with tongs. Add to soup and cook until squash is very tender.

Stir in honey, sage, thyme, and salt and pepper to taste. Purée in food processor.

Garnish with Cinnamon Maple Cream and chopped cilantro.

SERVES 8

CINNAMON MAPLE CREAM

½ cup sour cream
½ teaspoon lime juice
1 teaspoon maple syrup
½ teaspoon cinnamon

Combine all ingredients and mix thoroughly.

AUTHOR'S NOTE: It may take four or five batches to purée this amount of soup. If a thicker bisque is desired, return the purée to the stock pot and simmer until it reaches the desired consistency.

~~~~~~~~~~~

Black Bean and Corn Soup

Eddie's Grill, Phoenix, Arizona

CHEF EDDIE MATNEY

1 onion, chopped
1 shallot, chopped
8 cloves garlic, chopped
¼ pound (1 stick) butter
2 pounds black beans
2 gallons vegetable stock (nineteen 13¾-ounce cans)
2 cups apple cider vinegar

OPPOSITE: *From top: Roasted Poblano Chile Soup (recipe page 16) and Butternut Squash Bisque with Cinnamon Maple Cream (recipe page 17)*

2 teaspoons celery salt

1 teaspoon pepper

Corn Mixture (recipe follows)

I n a large stock pot, cook onion, shallot, and garlic in butter until tender. Add beans and mix well so that each bean is coated with butter. Add remaining ingredients except corn mixture. Cover and simmer for 3 hours or until beans are soft. Stir in corn mixture and simmer an additional 20 minutes.

SERVES 8 TO 10

CORN MIXTURE

6 ears corn, husked and grilled

2 tablespoons chopped, roasted green chiles

2 tablespoons ground cumin

1 tablespoon chopped cilantro

1 red bell pepper, chopped

C ut corn from cobs. In a bowl, combine corn kernels with chiles, cumin, cilantro, and red pepper.

YIELDS 2 CUPS

AUTHOR'S NOTE: If corn is not in season, roast frozen corn under a broiler. See "Vegetable Stocks," pages 124 to 125, for more information on preparing stocks.

FENNEL

NO ONE IS sure just where fennel cultivation started or how fennel moved across the continents. However, fennel was available to early North American inhabitants long before Europeans arrived. Native Americans used it as a snack, as an addition to other dishes, and as an additive to mask the flavors of bitter medicinal herbs. Fennel flavor is familiar to most people, even if they have never seen a fennel bulb. There is a sweet overtone of licorice, much of which softens with cooking. The shoots can be eaten like celery and the bulb cut and added to many dishes.

Fennel appears round and hearty. It should have fresh green stalks and round, unblemished bulbs. Fennel will easily keep in a plastic bag in the refrigerator for 3 to 5 days with little loss of flavor. Fennel is very low in calories and extremely rich in vitamin A.

Basic preparation includes cutting off the stalks (they are good for snacking) and the hard base. Peel off the outer layer of the bulb, then quarter and slice the bulb like an onion.

To boil fennel, place it in a covered saucepan with just enough water to cover, bring to a boil, and cook, covered, for 7 to 10 minutes. For added flavor, use bouillon instead of water or enhance the water with salt and butter. Drain the fennel and toss it with an herb of your choice and even a bit of olive oil. Serve immediately.

If you would rather sauté fennel, do so as you would any other vegetable, with butter or oil in a medium-warm skillet. Cook for about 10 minutes and serve with sautéed onions or garlic for a real treat.

Parsnip and Fennel Soup
with Cheese Diablotin

Razz's Restaurant and Bar,
Scottsdale, Arizona

CHEF ERASMO "RAZZ" KAMNITZER

PARSNIP AND FENNEL SOUP

- 2 tablespoons butter
- 1 large onion, chopped
- 2 stalks celery, chopped
- 1 pound parsnips, peeled and chopped
- 1 pound fennel bulb, chopped
- 2 tablespoons flour
- 5 cups vegetable stock (about three 13¾-ounce cans)
- 1 cup heavy cream
- 1 apple, chopped (optional)

Salt and pepper to taste

- 1 teaspoon red chile paste

In a heavy stock pot over medium heat, melt butter and sauté onion, celery, parsnips, and fennel until soft but not brown. Add the flour and stir continually for approximately 2 minutes. Add the vegetable stock and the apple, bring to a boil, and simmer for approximately 20 minutes. Add the cream and apple and cook for 5 more minutes. Let cool, then purée in a blender. Season with salt, pepper, and red chile paste to taste. Serve with Cheese Diablotin (recipe follows).

SERVES 4 TO 6

CHEESE DIABLOTIN

2 eggs, separated

¼ cup mayonnaise

¼ cup grated Parmesan cheese

¼ cup shredded Cheddar cheese

1 tablespoon finely sliced fresh chives

1 tablespoon chopped onion

1 tablespoon chopped fresh parsley (or 1 teaspoon dried)

1 tablespoon chopped fresh marjoram (or 1 teaspoon dried)

1 tablespoon chopped fresh tarragon (or 1 teaspoon dried)

16 to 24 baguette slices

In a large bowl, mix egg yolks, mayonnaise, Parmesan and Cheddar cheeses, chives, onion, parsley, marjoram, and tarragon. Set aside.

Preheat oven to 350 degrees.

In a small bowl, whip the egg whites until stiff but not dry and fold into the cheese mixture. Top each slice of bread with 1 to 2 tablespoons of this mixture. Place on a baking sheet. Bake for 10 to 15 minutes or until golden brown. Serve on top of Parsnip Fennel Soup.

AUTHOR'S NOTE: Razz Kamnitzer says that to make this soup strictly vegetarian all one has to do is omit the cream from the soup and substitute soybean cheese and eggless mayonnaise in the diablotin. Margarine or oil may be substituted for butter.

Tomatillo Soup

Garland's Oak Creek Lodge,
Sedona, Arizona

CHEF AMANDA STINE

3 stalks celery, sliced

1 large leek, white and tender green, sliced

2 medium carrots, sliced

½ cup seeded and diced red bell pepper

½ cup seeded and diced yellow bell pepper

¼ cup seeded and diced poblano chile

2 cups sliced tomatillos, husks removed

1 tablespoon olive oil

1 teaspoon dried oregano

1 teaspoon dried thyme

1 teaspoon dried sage

1 tablespoon ground cumin

1 tablespoon ground red chile

1 teaspoon kosher salt

6 cups water

⅓ cup fresh orange juice

¼ cup fresh lime juice

¼ cup chopped cilantro

In large pan over medium heat, sauté the celery, leek, carrots, bell peppers, poblano, and tomatillos in olive oil. Add oregano, thyme, sage, cumin, red chile, and salt. Add water to cover and simmer until tender. Add juices and cilantro. Season with salt to taste.

SERVES 6

AUTHOR'S NOTE: Soup keeps well and tastes very good the second and even third day after preparation, so don't hesitate to make this early.

MAKING A ROUX

SEVERAL RECIPES IN this book call for "roux," a combination of flour and butter used as a thickener. From this humble beginning, many additional ingredients may be added to create a thickener with its own character. A white sauce might be made with milk, a brown sauce with red wine and beef stock. For vegetarian cooks, equal parts of flour and butter will create a starter as delicious as any. The secret is blending and cooking the roux properly.

Begin with equal amounts of butter and flour. Over medium heat, melt the butter in a saucepan, being careful not to let the butter burn. When completely melted, add the flour slowly, then whisk rapidly to incorporate all the flour into the butter and to remove all lumps. As the roux is blending, it is cooking—and browning. The whole process takes about three minutes. The pastelike roux can be used immediately, or covered and refrigerated for up to two weeks.

It doesn't take much roux to thicken sauces or soups. For example, a cup of liquid will thicken noticeably with a roux made from only one tablespoon of flour and one tablespoon of butter.

The best results are obtained by using clarified butter, which is butter with the milk solids removed. This produces lighter sauces and roux. To clarify butter, melt it in a saucepan, being careful not to brown it. When the butter is fully melted, skim off the foam and pour the remaining liquid into a bowl. Discard the remaining fat solids left behind. Clarified butter will keep in the refrigerator just like regular butter.

Tortilla Soup

La Casa Sena Restaurant and Cantina, Santa Fe, New Mexico

CHEF KELLY ROGERS

¼ pound (1 stick) butter

½ cup flour

½ red onion, diced

2 cups diced tomatoes

3 cloves garlic, minced

2 cups prepared black beans

1 cup red chile sauce

1 cup green chile sauce

½ gallon vegetable stock (about 4½ 13¾-ounce cans)

2 cups corn kernels

2 tablespoons chopped cilantro

2 tablespoons lime juice

4 corn tortillas, ground to meal

Aged jack cheese for garnish

Crispy fried tortillas for garnish

Make a roux with the butter and flour. Sauté the onion, tomatos, and garlic in the roux. Add the beans and the chile sauces. Add the stock and bring the soup to a simmering boil. Add the corn, cilantro, lime juice, and tortilla meal. Season and serve with cheese and crispy fried tortillas.

If you don't want to make chile sauces, use 2 tablespoons red chili powder and ½ cup chopped, peeled green chile, and increase the roux by a half and the stock by 2 cups.

SERVES 4 TO 6

AUTHOR'S NOTE: The chef says this recipe incorporates several tastes of New Mexican cuisine.

Black Bean Chili and Roasted Corn Soup

Cafe Terra Cotta, Scottsdale, Arizona

CHEF CHRISTOPHER T. WHITE

- 3 pounds black beans
- 1 small yellow onion, chopped
- 3 tablespoons olive oil
- 1 large tomato, chopped
- 2 teaspoons chopped fresh garlic
- 1 small green bell pepper, seeded and chopped
- 1 poblano chile, seeded and chopped
- 1 jalapeño chile, seeded and diced
- 1 dried ancho chile, rehydrated and chopped
- 1½ tablespoons cumin seed
- 2 tablespoons dried oregano
- 1 teaspoon cayenne
- 2 teaspoons paprika
- 1 bay leaf

Water to cover

- 4 cups roasted fresh corn on the cob
- 1 teaspoon fresh lime juice
- 1 bunch cilantro, coarsely chopped (reserving 8 sprigs for garnish)
- 4 cups spicy vegetable broth (vegetable broth simmered with 1 to 3 chiles of your choice)
- 1 ounce balsamic vinegar

Salt and pepper to taste

- 1 cup sour cream for garnish

oak black beans overnight so they are ready when you assemble the chili and soup. When beans are ready, set aside.

In a large stock pot, sauté onion in olive oil until soft. Add the tomato, garlic, bell pepper, and chiles and cook until tender. Add soaked beans, cumin seed, oregano, cayenne, paprika, bay leaf, and water to cover by 3 inches. Cook, uncovered, over medium heat until beans are tender, adding more water if necessary. Drain, remove bay leaf, and blend with remaining ingredients. Garnish with sour cream and cilantro. Serve at once.

SERVES 8 TO 12

AUTHOR'S NOTE: If unable to roast whole ears of corn, skip the roasting step and simply substitute 4 cups fresh, frozen, or well-drained canned corn.

Cooking times for the black bean chili are highly variable depending on size, freshness, et cetera. Cook until tender, and expect this to take at least an hour.

If you are unable to find all the chiles indicated in this recipe, feel free to add or delete as you see fit.

~~~~~~~~~

Southwestern "Yellow" Gazpacho

Prairie Star, Santa Ana Golf Club, Bernalillo, New Mexico

CHEF JAN K. LEITHE

8 ripe yellow tomatoes
2 yellow bell peppers, coarsely chopped
8 tomatillos, coarsely chopped
3 serrano chiles, coarsely chopped
1 clove garlic

½ cup finely diced red onion

¼ cup finely chopped cilantro

¼ cup olive oil

¼ cup balsamic vinegar

½ teaspoon salt

¼ teaspoon black pepper

¼ teaspoon cayenne pepper

1 cup ice (crushed, if possible)

Core the tomatoes, parcook in boiling salted water, cool immediately in ice water, and remove the skins. Combine the tomatoes, bell peppers, tomatillos, serranos, and garlic and divide into two batches, then purée in a food processor. Place in a mixing bowl, add red onion, cilantro, olive oil, balsamic vinegar, salt, pepper, cayenne, and ice. Mix well and season to taste. Garnish with an edible flower, if desired, such as squash blossoms. This gazpacho is best served one day after preparation.

SERVES 6 TO 8

AUTHOR'S NOTE: This very straightforward recipe offers great opportunity to substitute without seriously affecting the wonderful blend of flavors Chef Jan created. Red tomatoes can be used for yellow if unavailable, and green bell peppers can be substituted for yellow. Adjust cayenne to suit your own level of "heat"!

BEANS

Beans can be traced as a food source to at least 15,000 years ago. In the Southwest, both the Hopi and Zuni used them in ceremony. The thousand or so varieties of beans now available comprise a food source high in protein. Combined with a grain, beans provide an excellent source of complete protein.

Sort beans carefully. Discard broken and wrinkled beans and other debris, then place them in a large pot. Add water, swish the beans, and discard any beans or debris that float to the top. Wash the remaining beans well.

Soaking will soften harder beans and reduce cooking time. Although beans are not marked with an expiration date, older beans must soak longer than fresher ones, so it is best to estimate on the high side to ensure they are completely softened. Soaking anywhere from three to ten hours should finish the task. For soaks longer than three hours, refrigerate the beans in the soaking pot to prevent spoilage.

To shorten the soaking cycle, parboil the beans. Cover them with about two inches of cold water and bring to a boil for three to five minutes. Then turn off the heat and let the beans rest in the hot liquid for another hour or two. For very sensitive digestive systems, draining can be done twice with some benefit.

Beans come in differing degrees of hardness, so cooking time varies. Quick-cooking beans are usually the smaller, softer beans, like lentils and split peas. Black, kidney, pinto, and navy beans take longer to cook. Garbanzos and soybeans require both lengthy soaking and additional cooking time.

About 1 cup of dried beans equals 2½ cups of soaked beans. If not cooking them immediately, refrigerate beans after soaking.

Anasazi

Black

Black-eyed Peas

Garbanzo

Kidney

Lentil

Lima

Soy

Northern

Red

Roasted Garlic, Mushroom, and Broccoli Dumplings in Gingered Broth

Michael's at the Citadel, Scottsdale, Arizona

CHEF MICHAEL J. DEMARIA

GINGERED BROTH

2 tablespoons sesame oil

¼ cup chopped white onion

1 cup peeled and chopped fresh ginger

½ cup chopped celery

½ cup chopped carrots

1 bulb garlic, minced

1 tablespoon black peppercorns, cracked

4 bay leaves

2 tablespoons salt

½ cup chardonnay

1½ quarts (6 cups) water

Dumplings (recipe follows)

Garnish (recipe follows)

Over medium-high heat in a hot, heavy-bottomed stock pot, sauté the sesame oil and onion for 2 minutes. Add the ginger, celery, carrots, garlic, peppercorns, bay leaves, and salt and sauté for 5 minutes over medium heat, allowing the flavors and aromas to release from the vegetables. Deglaze the pan with the chardonnay and cook for

OPPOSITE: *Clockwise from upper left: Roasted Garlic, Mushroom, and Broccoli Dumplings in Gingered Broth, Southwestern "Yellow" Gazpacho (recipe page 28), and Black Bean Chili and Roasted Corn Soup (recipe page 27)*

4 to 5 minutes. Add the water and bring to a boil, then reduce heat and let simmer until reduced by one-third. Purée the stock and strain it through a very fine strainer lined with a coffee filter. This process will take awhile, but it will produce a clear broth. Keep hot until ready to cook dumplings and garnish, or store overnight in the refrigerator.

To serve, bring the broth to a simmer in a wok or stock pot. Add the dumplings and cook them until the wontons are tender. Add the shiitake mushrooms. Garnish and pour into serving bowls.

SERVES 6 TO 8

ROASTED GARLIC, MUSHROOM, AND BROCCOLI DUMPLINGS

3 bulbs garlic
1 tablespoon olive oil
2 heads broccoli
3 tablespoons butter
Salt and pepper to taste
1 package of wonton skins
1 pound shiitake mushrooms, stems removed
Sesame oil for sautéing vegetables

Preheat oven to 375 degrees.

To prepare garlic, cut off the top of each bulb. Rub them lightly with olive oil and roast them for 30 minutes. Let cool. When cooled, squeeze out the roasted garlic and set aside.

Snip tiny florets off the broccoli heads, reserving the stems. Blanch the florets in boiling water, then place them in ice water. Once cold, strain and set aside. Prepare the broccoli stems by cutting about 2 inches off the bottoms and discarding them. Chop the remaining stems into ¼-inch pieces and sauté them in the butter. Add the roasted garlic and cook for about 5 minutes, until the broccoli is bright green and tender. Purée.

In a bowl, combine the broccoli florets and garlic-broccoli purée. Season to taste. Lay out the wonton skins and spoon about ½ teaspoon of the stuffing on the center of each wonton skin. Wet the edges and pull them up to the middle to form ruffled-top dumplings. Set aside.

Slice the shiitake mushrooms into julienne strips and sauté them in the sesame oil until tender. Set aside.

GARNISH

> 2 tablespoons finely chopped fresh ginger
> 2 tablespoons finely chopped lemon grass
> 2 tablespoons chopped cilantro
> 4 tablespoons bias-cut scallions

AUTHOR'S NOTE: See "deglazing" in the glossary for more information about this process.

Be sure to save the strained vegetables and add them to a vegetable stock or use them as a garnish on salads.

~~~~~~~~~~~~~

White Corn and Chipotle Soup

The Range Cafe, Bernalillo, New Mexico

CHEF JAY D. WULF

> 3 ears fresh white sweet corn
> 5 cups water
> 2 pinches kosher salt
> 2 tablespoons butter, or margarine or salad oil
> 1½ cups diced onion
> ¾ cup chopped celery
> 3 chipotle peppers, seeded and diced
> 2 medium-size russet potatoes, peeled and coarsely chopped
> Freshly ground black pepper to taste
> Fresh cilantro sprigs for garnish
> Lime juice for garnish

GARLIC

ALMOST 90 PERCENT of domestic garlic is grown in the western United States, and it has woven its way into many Southwestern dishes. Garlic is from the lily family and is a single bulb containing many cloves. One clove of garlic contains but 1 calorie. Bulbs are grown almost all year and harvested when the tops begin to dry out.

Egyptian slaves, some of whom spent much of their lives sliding huge rocks to assemble pyramids, ate onions and garlic as staples. However, garlic has played a far greater role in history as a medicine. It was used to cure toothaches by stuffing the tooth cavity with a clove. It was also used to treat dog bites and as a preventive for overconsumption.

Today garlic is available as whole cloves, powdered, granulated, or minced. Powdered and granulated forms are pure garlic; garlic salt is mixed with table salt. These dried garlic products are best if no more than six months old.

For fresh whole cloves, choose plump and firm bulbs with unbroken skin.

To use fresh garlic, break off a clove from the bulb and remove the skin. To peel, lay a clove on a solid surface and mash it with the flat side of a knife. Use it whole, chopped, minced, or pressed. A garlic press will promote the most powerful flavoring, but discard the residual pulp inside the press. The garlic passed through the press will flavor a dish nicely. Cooking generally moderates garlic's strong, pungent odor.

To store, keep whole, fresh garlic bulbs in a cool, dry, airy place, and do not refrigerate. Leave the heads as intact as possible or the entire bulb will dry out quickly. They will last about three months.

huck and clean corn, and reserve corn cobs after removing kernels. Place the corn cobs in a pot large enough to hold them. Cover them with water, add a pinch of salt, and bring to a slow simmer, uncovered, for 20 to 30 minutes. Remove cobs, strain stock, and set liquid aside.

In a stock pot, melt the butter over low heat. Add corn kernels, onion, celery, and a pinch of salt and cook, uncovered, for 3 to 5 minutes. Add chipotle peppers, potatoes, and stock. Simmer until the potatoes are cooked through. Purée all ingredients and adjust consistency with a little water if too thick. Add ground pepper and adjust salt if necessary. To serve, pour into bowls and garnish with cilantro sprigs and a squeeze of lime.

SERVES 2 TO 4

AUTHOR'S NOTE: If corn is not in season, use frozen corn and a quart of vegetable stock for the water.

Oven-Roasted Tomato Soup with Lime-Cilantro Crema

Seasons Grill, Durango, Colorado

CHEF AMY NORBY

OVEN-ROASTED TOMATO SOUP

10 pounds ripe plum tomatoes
¼ cup olive oil
10 large cloves garlic, peeled
1 quart heavy cream or half-and-half
1 tablespoon lime juice
¼ cup chopped fresh basil

2 tablespoons chopped fresh dill (or 2 teaspoons dried)

Salt and pepper to taste

Preheat oven to 450 degrees. Toss the tomatoes with the olive oil and the garlic cloves and place them in a single layer in a large roasting pan. Roast tomatoes for approximately 45 minutes, or until the tomato skins are blistered and slightly blackened. Cool the tomatoes to room temperature.

Purée the roasted tomatoes and garlic in a blender or food processor, and then force the purée through a sieve to remove all seeds and skin from the purée.

Add heavy cream or half-and-half, the lime juice, basil, and dill. Season with salt and pepper to taste.

To serve, reheat soup to just below boiling temperature. Top with a large dollop of Lime-Cilantro Crema (recipe follows).

SERVES 4 TO 6

LIME-CILANTRO CREMA

1 cup sour cream

Juice of 2 limes

½ teaspoon salt

¼ teaspoon pepper

1 bunch fresh cilantro, leaves only, finely chopped

Stir all ingredients together.

Tomatillo Broth

Top of the Rock, The Buttes Resort, Tempe, Arizona

CHEF KURT ZÜGER

½ cup vegetable stock

1½ teaspoons cornstarch mixed with 3 tablespoons
   cold vegetable stock

1 pound tomatillos, husked and chopped

½ bunch cilantro, chopped

½ jalapeño, seeded and chopped or minced

1½ teaspoons minced garlic

1 teaspoon lime juice

½ teaspoon sugar

½ teaspoon salt

Bring the vegetable stock to a boil and thicken to desired consistency with cornstarch mixture. Add remaining ingredients and cook for 5 minutes. In a blender or food processor, purée soup until smooth. Strain and serve.

SERVES 6

AVOCADOS

THE AVOCADO REMAINS a favorite ingredient of Mexican and other Southwestern meals. Avocados were cultivated by the early Aztec and Mayan farmers of the territory, long before the arrival of the Spanish. Also known as alligator pears, avocados are now grown throughout Mexico and southern California and represent a significant cash crop.

Avocados found on grocery shelves are usually the larger pear-shaped variety. They are a rusty green in color and just beginning to soften when ready to use. Avocado's peak season is from December through April, but they are available most of the year, if a bit more expensive.

When shopping for just the right avocado, select one with uniform skin color that yields to light pressure. If you see bruises or punctures, put it back. Firmer avocados will take two to three days to ripen. Never place avocados in the refrigerator unless they are ripe; then they will last up to two weeks.

As for nutritive value, avocados are not at the top of the chain as a popular diet food. Although they contain vitamin C, thiamine, and riboflavin, they are generally denounced for their high fat content. Unfortunately, as good as avocados may taste, they can contain as much as 20 percent fat and 160 to 170 calories each. However, used in moderation, avocados are quite a treat.

Chilled Avocado Soup

Las Ventanas, Scottsdale Princess Resort, Scottsdale, Arizona

CHEF REED GROBAN

1 jalapeño, seeded and finely chopped

1 teaspoon finely chopped garlic

⅓ cup finely chopped cilantro leaves

2 scallions, finely chopped

Juice of two limes

1 teaspoon salt

1 teaspoon ground cumin

3 avocados, skinned and seeded

2 cups low-fat plain yogurt, plus 8 tablespoons for garnish

2 cups V-8 or tomato juice

Approximately 2 cups cold water

Fresh cilantro leaves for garnish

Chopped tomatoes for garnish

In a food processor bowl, combine jalapeño, garlic, cilantro, scallions, lime juice, salt, cumin, and avocados. Process ingredients at high speed until the consistency of a smooth paste. Continue processing on high speed, adding 2 cups of the yogurt, the V-8 juice, and as much water as needed to produce a medium-thick consistency. Chill 3 to 4 hours before serving.

To serve, pour soup into bowls, garnishing with a dollop of yogurt, fresh cilantro leaves, and chopped tomatoes.

SERVES 6 TO 8

AUTHOR'S NOTE: Quick and easy, this is a thick soup. It can be served warm if desired.

Tofu-Tortilla Soup

Golden Swan, Hyatt Regency, Scottsdale, Arizona

CHEF ANTON BRUNBAUER

2 medium red onions, cut into ¼-inch cubes

1 medium jicama, peeled and cut into ¼-inch cubes

1 medium carrot, peeled and cut into ¼-inch cubes

2 medium green peppers, seeded and sliced
   into ½-inch cubes

1 large tomato, cut into ¼-inch cubes

2 dry chipotle chiles, chopped

2½ quarts water or vegetable stock

¾ cup miso paste

¼ cup soy sauce

3 tablespoons chopped fresh cilantro

Cumin to taste

1 pound tofu, cut into ½-inch cubes

Corn tortillas, fried or baked and cut into julienne strips

Combine onion, jicama, carrot, green peppers, tomato, chipotles, water, miso paste, soy sauce, cilantro, and cumin. Bring to a boil, lower heat to medium, and cook for 10 to 12 minutes. Add tofu and simmer for 2 more minutes. Serve in soup bowls and garnish with tortilla strips.

SERVES 6

AUTHOR'S NOTE: See the glossary for more information about miso paste. Some testers of this recipe have added their favorite herbs and spices to those listed. This is an excellent base for other flavorings. Try other herbs for a change of pace.

TOFU

MANY NEWCOMERS TO a healthy diet are often confused about tofu. As a compressed soybean-milk curd, tofu first appears as appealing as, well, a compressed soybean-milk curd. However, custardlike tofu has been the staple of many Asian diets for hundreds of years. Now it is being consumed in the United States, and we haven't scratched the surface of tofu's potential.

As abundant as tofu is, its development is obscure. What can be surmised is that soybeans were cultivated in Asia for their yield per acre, for nothing else produced as much protein in such small acreage.

The Western world with its wide-open pastures had no such concerns. Although steers eat twenty times more protein than they produce in steaks, it was of little consequence in a new frontier.

But what a different time makes. Tofu is now a supermarket norm, found fresh in boxes bedded in water, as a powder in packets, and whole in cans. It is one of the few foods served fried, broiled, baked, sautéed, scrambled, or simmered. As a stand-alone product, tofu is bland. However, it absorbs whatever flavors it contacts.

Tofu is embraced by health-food advocates because of its astounding nutritional properties. It is loaded with vitamins and minerals, low in calories and saturated fat, and contains no cholesterol. All this and packed with protein too: It's a wonder it's not sold at every fast-food counter in the country.

When taken out of its wrapping, fresh tofu spoils in a matter of days, so buy it only when needed.

Cream of Sweet Red Pepper Soup

The Ranchers Club of New Mexico, Albuquerque Hilton, Albuquerque, New Mexico

CHEF RICHARD C. PERALES

¼ pound (1 stick) butter

5 red bell peppers, roasted, peeled, and seeded

½ jalapeño, seeded and diced

1 shallot, diced

1 bunch fresh cilantro, leaves only

1 cup Chablis

2 cups vegetable stock

2 cloves garlic, minced

½ teaspoon fennel seed, fresh or dried

1 quart heavy cream

¼ cup honey

In a large saucepan, melt butter over medium heat. Add peppers, jalapeño, shallot, and cilantro and sauté for 10 minutes. Add wine and reduce to ⅛ liquid. Add vegetable stock and let simmer for 10 minutes. Add garlic and fennel to soup and stir well for about 5 minutes. Remove from heat.

Place the cooked mixture in a food processor or blender and purée until smooth. Run the purée through a fine strainer and stir vigorously with a whip to encourage it through the strainer. Discard anything left in the strainer, saving all the liquid possible.

Place heavy cream in the saucepan and reduce it at a light boil until thickened. Add the strained purée to the cream and stir with a whip to combine. Add honey and allow the liquid to thicken, uncovered, to the consistency you want. The more you cook this soup, the thicker and darker it gets. Serve hot.

SERVES 6

AUTHOR'S NOTE: After straining vegetables, save whatever is left in the strainer. It is delicious on crackers or blended in another recipe.

Mesquite-Roasted Yellow Tomato Soup with Piñon-Cilantro Pesto and Crispy Potato Curls

Inn of the Anasazi, Santa Fe, New Mexico

CHEF FLYNT PAYNE

MESQUITE-ROASTED YELLOW TOMATO SOUP

12 yellow tomatoes, chopped

3 cloves garlic, minced

1 medium onion, diced

½ cup balsamic vinegar

Juice and zest of 2 lemons

½ cup honey

1 chipotle chile, ground

1 quart heavy cream

1 cup buttermilk

Salt and pepper to taste

Pinch of saffron

½ to 1 cup apple juice (optional)

½ cup crumbled feta cheese

Pesto (recipe follows)

Potato curls (recipe follows)

Cilantro leaves for garnish

½ to 1 cup apple juice (optional)

Heat a grill over some mesquite, then grill tomatoes until they are soft. Add them to a stock pot with garlic, onion, vinegar, lemon juice and zest, honey, and chipotle. Cook over low heat for 20 minutes. Add cream, buttermilk, salt, pepper, and saffron, and cook for 30 minutes. Taste and adjust seasonings. If thinning is needed, add apple juice.

To serve, pour soup into bowls and place a pinch of feta cheese in the center. Drizzle pesto around the cheese. Top each serving with a fried potato curl and a cilantro leaf.

PIÑON-CILANTRO PESTO

1 cup roasted piñon nuts
1 bunch cilantro
1 teaspoon toasted and ground coriander seeds
1 clove garlic
¾ cup asiago cheese
1 cup olive oil
Salt to taste

Combine piñon nuts, cilantro, coriander, garlic, and cheese in a food processor and process well. Add oil and salt and process well again.

CRISPY POTATO CURLS

2 Yukon Gold potatoes
Vegetable oil for frying (½ inch on bottom of pan)

Use a potato peeler to peel each potato lengthwise in a continuous "curl," allowing the curl to drop into a bowl filled with cold water. Heat the oil to 375 degrees, drain and dry the curls to avoid splattering, and fry them until golden. Drain curls on paper towels.

AUTHOR'S NOTE: This soup tastes even better the second day. If yellow tomatoes are not available, use ripened red ones.

Although potato curls are optional, they make a wonderful presentation.

Asiago cheese is a delight but use Parmesan if not available.

SERVES 4 TO 6

EGGPLANT

EGGPLANT WAS FIRST GROWN in the East Indies but made its way to Spain in the Middle Ages. Dubbed the "mad apple," this small, oval, pale fruit was blamed for having caused problems from digestive-tract ailments to madness. A few brave cooks persevered until eggplant became palatable for the masses. Through mass cultivation, the eggplant eventually became the oblong fruit we now see in the produce bin.

Eggplant is very low in calories: about 8 per ounce. It is also very low in nutritional value, but can add volume and variety to a dish without adding dietary woes.

Look for eggplant that is heavy, firm, smooth, and uniform in color. Avoid bruised specimens. Large, rough, spongy places on the eggplant are not good. If dark-brown spots appear on the skin, the shelf life is at an end.

Refrigerate eggplant for maximum shelf life, which is only three to four days. If it's on the edge, cook it immediately: It should last another three to four days.

Wash and slice eggplant just before you're ready to cook it. Although the recipes in this book call for peeling, don't worry about assembling a dish with the outer skin intact, for much of the flavor is in the skin.

Boil eggplant for 10 minutes in ½ inch of salted water. Pan fry it for 5 to 10 minutes in light oil. For the most fat-free solution, bake it for 20 to 30 minutes at 350 degrees. You can even broil eggplant for 10 minutes if you like. To deep fry (dieters, skip the next part), turn the fryer up to 380 degrees, bread eggplant if desired, and immerse in hot oil for 8 to 10 minutes.

Smoky Eggplant Soup

Café de las Placitas,
Placitas, New Mexico

CHEF MATTHEW BESSE-BREWER

4 eggplants, peeled and cut into large cubes

2 tablespoons kosher salt

4 red bell peppers, seeded and cut in half

1 tablespoon olive oil, plus some for brushing on vegetables

1 gallon vegetable stock (about 9½ 13¾-ounce cans)

2 onions, sliced

1 leek, white part only, sliced

1 fennel bulb, sliced

1 bulb garlic, roasted, skinned, and chopped

½ cup sun-dried tomatoes, reconstituted and chopped

½ tablespoon chopped fresh thyme (or ½ teaspoon dried)

1 tablespoon chopped fresh basil (or 1 teaspoon dried)

½ cup grated Parmesan

3 tablespoons balsamic vinegar

½ tablespoon ground fennel seed

Salt and pepper to taste

Toss eggplant with kosher salt in a colander and let stand for 1 hour to leach excess water. Heat a grill or barbecue (adding a few smoke chips or mesquite to your grill will enhance the soup's flavor). If using an oven, preheat to 400 degrees. Pat excess water and salt off the eggplant. Brush eggplant and peppers with a little olive oil and grill until tender.

Simmer vegetable stock for 15 minutes. Sauté onions, leek, and fennel and pour in vegetable stock. Add eggplant and red pepper, garlic, tomatoes, and thyme. Simmer for an additional 30 minutes. Purée soup in a blender and add basil, Parmesan, balsamic vinegar, and fennel seed. Adjust salt, pepper, and seasonings as needed.

SERVES 6 TO 8

Entrées

Entrées should present elements of both presentation and pleasant tastes, as they are the core of any meal. One of the many refreshing surprises our testers found when making the dishes for this book was the multitude of wonderful flavors they had never experienced. The combinations of vegetables and spices that contributing chefs developed for these recipes have opened new vistas for many palates.

Many of these entrées can be used as a side dish to other entrées, or served in smaller portions for a delightful appetizer. They are that versatile!

Grilled Vegetable Flautas with Chile Tomato Sauce and Salsa Verde

Copper Queen Hotel, Bisbee, Arizona

CHEF JOHN DALOIA

GRILLED VEGETABLE FLAUTAS

    2 cups olive oil
    ½ cup soy sauce
    1 tablespoon chopped garlic
    1 tablespoon chopped shallots
    2 medium zucchini, sliced
    2 medium yellow squash, sliced
    1 large red bell pepper, seeded and sliced into strips
    1 large green bell pepper, seeded and sliced into strips
    1 medium red onion, chopped
    1 bunch asparagus, sliced into ½-inch pieces
    8 (10-inch) flour tortillas
    2 cups cooked black beans
    2 cups grated Monterey jack cheese
    ½ cup sour cream for garnish
    Finely chopped jalapeños for garnish (optional)

Combine the olive oil, soy sauce, garlic, and shallots. Add the zucchini, yellow squash, bell peppers, onion, and asparagus and marinate overnight. The next day, grill the vegetables over hot coals until done but still crisp. Dice the cooked vegetables into ½-inch pieces.

Preheat oven to 350 degrees.

Heat tortillas in a hot skillet until marked but still soft. In the center of each tortilla, place some of the grilled vegetables plus 1 heaping tablespoon each of the black beans and jack cheese. Roll as tight as you can without splitting the tortilla.

Place the rolled flautas in the oven and bake until centers are hot (15 to 20 minutes) and the cheese has melted. On one half of each plate, ladle some red chile tomato sauce, and on the other half place a tablespoon of the salsa verde. Serve two flautas per plate and garnish with a tablespoon of sour cream atop the flautas, and an optional sprinkling of finely chopped jalapeños.

SERVES 4

CHILE TOMATO SAUCE

- 6 large ripe tomatoes, chopped
- 1 large red bell pepper, seeded and chopped
- 1 large green bell pepper, seeded and chopped
- 1 medium yellow onion, chopped
- 1 tablespoon minced garlic
- 2 tablespoons olive oil
- 2 tablespoons ground cumin
- 2 tablespoons dark red chili powder
- 2 cups vegetable stock

Salt and pepper to taste

Sauté the tomatoes, bell peppers, onion, and garlic in the olive oil until soft. Add the cumin and chili powder and cook over low heat for 5 minutes. Add the stock and bring to a boil. Boil for 5 minutes, then purée the sauce until very smooth. Add salt and pepper to taste. Keep sauce warm.

SALSA VERDE

- 6 large tomatillos, husked and chopped
- 1 medium yellow onion, chopped
- 2 jalapeño peppers, chopped
- 2 tablespoons olive oil
- ½ cup vegetable stock

auté the tomatillos, onion, and jalapeños in olive oil until soft. Add the stock and bring to a boil. Simmer about 15 minutes. Purée until very smooth. Keep warm.

AUTHOR'S NOTE: Both sauces can be made a day ahead.

This recipe uses an abundance of vegetables, and you may have some left over. They will keep at least a day and are a delicious blend to use on top of salads or to make a stock.

~~~~~~~~~

Vegetables in Mole Verde

Cafe Poca Cosa, Tucson, Arizona

CHEF SUZANNA DAVILLA

Vegetable oil for frying tortillas (about ¼ inch in a
  heavy skillet)
6 corn tortillas, plus some to serve with the dish if desired
1 cup (about 5 ounces) sesame seeds
½ cup hulled, raw pumpkin seeds
⅓ cup shelled, natural pistachio nuts
⅓ cup blanched whole almonds
4 large garlic cloves
3 poblano chiles, chopped
4 serrano chiles, chopped
1½ cups chopped, husked tomatillos (about ½ pound)
1 large bunch fresh cilantro (about 2 cups packed),
  washed and dried
1 cup shredded greenleaf lettuce
About 4 cups vegetable broth
3 tablespoons safflower oil

MOLE

THE WORD "MOLE" comes from a Nahuatl Indian word meaning "sauce." Though there is considerable speculation about where mole was first created, it is believed the Aztecs are responsible for first mixing chiles in a sauce.

Sometimes incorrectly called a "Spanish sauce," mole is used over, and in, a number of Southwestern dishes. Its most notable ingredient is chocolate. Though many moles are made without chocolate, chocolate adds an unusual flavoring not found in any other sauce. Moles come in a variety of colors, including yellow, brown, red, green, and black, all depending on the chile base.

Moles are very popular among Southwestern chefs, not only because of the historical link to the indigenous tribes but also because they are so flexible. Virtually anything can be used as an ingredient in a mole. There are as many recipes for moles as there are cooks in Mexico.

You will find a number of mole recipes in this book. Feel free to use any one of them with any recipe. If mole preparation is too labor intensive for your tastes, you can purchase prepared moles in many Latino markets.

2 pounds mixed vegetables (such as spinach, zucchini, potatoes, carrots, green beans, summer squash), chopped and sautéed or steamed

Grated cheese of your choice to serve with vegetables (optional)

Heat vegetable oil over moderately high heat until hot but not smoking and fry tortillas in batches until golden brown on both sides. Transfer fried tortillas to paper towels to drain. Cool tortillas and break into pieces.

In a dry medium-size skillet, toast sesame seeds over moderate heat, stirring until golden brown, about 8 minutes. Transfer to a bowl to cool. Add pumpkin seeds to skillet and toast, stirring, until they puff up but do not darken, 2 to 3 minutes. Transfer pumpkin seeds to bowl with sesame seeds. Add pistachio nuts and almonds to skillet and toast until golden, 2 to 3 minutes. Transfer pistachio nuts and almonds to bowl with seed mixture and cool.

In a food processor, blend garlic, chiles, tomatillos, cilantro, lettuce, and tortilla pieces with 1½ to 2 cups of the broth until mixture forms a thick paste. Add seed-nut mixture and blend until sauce is combined well but not smooth.

In a large saucepan, heat safflower oil over moderate heat until hot and add sauce. Cook sauce over moderate heat, stirring frequently, adding remaining broth as necessary to reach a thick, pasty consistency, about 12 minutes.

Stir vegetables into mixture and cook for about 10 minutes. Serve mole and vegetables with grated cheese and warmed corn tortillas, if desired.

SERVES 6 TO 8

AUTHOR'S NOTE: Chef Suzanna Davilla says this recipe is also delicious as a pie. Line the bottom of a pie plate with fried, but not crisp, corn tortillas. Add half the vegetables and half the mole and top with a grated cheese such as jack. Lay down another layer of corn tortillas, the remaining vegetables and mole, and top with more cheese. Bake until cheese is melted. Serve warm and slice like a pie.

Polenta and Pine Nut–Stuffed Red Peppers with Mole

High Desert Inn, Bisbee, Arizona

CHEF MARGARET HARTNETT

4 cups water

1 tablespoon salt

2 teaspoons black pepper

1 tablespoon ground cumin

2 cups uncooked polenta

½ cup diced scallions

1 tablespoon chopped oregano, (or 1½ teaspoons dried)

½ cup pine nuts, toasted

1 (4-ounce) can green chiles, diced

1½ cups grated Monterey jack cheese

4 red bell peppers, tops removed and seeded

4 to 8 slices sweet onion (especially red, white, Vidalia,
    or Walla Wallas)

12 large zucchini, sliced

Vegetable oil to coat vegetables

Mole sauce

Bring water to boil, add salt, pepper, and cumin, then reduce heat and slowly add polenta, stirring constantly until all is added and water is absorbed. Remove from heat, stir in scallions, oregano, pine nuts, green chiles, and 1 cup of the grated cheese.

Preheat oven to 350 degrees.

Fill red peppers with polenta mixture and place in a nonstick or oiled roasting pan. Bake for 20 to 25 minutes, remove and top with

OPPOSITE: *From top: Pepper-Corn Muffins (recipe page 144) and Polenta and Pine Nut–Stuffed Red Peppers with Mole*

remaining cheese, then bake until cheese is melted. While peppers are baking, lightly oil onion and zucchini slices and grill. To serve, cover plate bottom with mole sauce, place one pepper in the center, and surround with grilled onions and zucchini.

SERVES 4

AUTHOR'S NOTES: Prepared mole is available in many markets, or use one of the mole recipes in this book. Also, see "Mole," page 54.

~~~~~~~~~~

Green Chile–Quinoa Casserole

Top of Sedona, Sedona, Arizona

CHEF COREY ERWIN

1 (12-ounce) box quinoa
Cooking spray or vegetable oil to coat sauté pan and
    baking dish
1 tablespoon chopped garlic
1 bunch scallions, chopped
1 medium white onion, diced
1 (10-ounce) can spicy tomatoes with green chiles
1 (15-ounce) can pinto beans, drained and rinsed
1½ teaspoons ground cumin
½ teaspoon salt
½ teaspoon dried oregano
½ teaspoon chili powder
1 teaspoon sugar
Four 8-inch flour tortillas
1 (4-ounce) can whole green chiles, cut into strips
4 ounces shredded Monterey jack cheese
2 ounces shredded Cheddar cheese
1 bunch cilantro, chopped

Cook quinoa in water or vegetable stock according to package instructions. Set aside.

Coat a large sauté pan with cooking spray or vegetable oil and place over medium heat until hot. Add garlic, scallions, and onion and sauté until translucent, stirring occasionally. Stir in tomatoes, pinto beans, cumin, salt, oregano, chili powder, and sugar and simmer for an additional 5 minutes.

Preheat oven to 325 degrees.

Coat a 13 x 9 x 2-inch baking dish with cooking spray. Arrange tortillas in dish and top with tomato mixture. Cover with cooled quinoa and green chile strips. Cover and bake for 25 minutes or until thoroughly heated. Sprinkle with shredded cheeses and cilantro. Bake an additional 5 minutes to melt cheeses. Serve with your favorite salsa or sour cream.

SERVES 6 TO 8

Yavapai Vegetarian Chili

Enchantment Resort, Sedona, Arizona

CHEF KEVIN E. MAGUIRE

2 large eggplants, peeled and diced

1½ tablespoons kosher salt

¾ cup olive oil

1 large onion, diced

2 tablespoons minced garlic

2 large green bell peppers, seeded and diced

2 pounds canned tomatoes, including juice

1½ pounds fresh tomatoes, diced

2 tablespoons chili powder

1 tablespoon dried ground cumin

1 tablespoon dried oregano

1 tablespoon dried basil

1 tablespoon freshly ground black pepper

½ cup fennel seed

½ cup chopped fresh parsley

1 cup Anasazi beans (soaked overnight)

1 cup garbanzo beans (if fresh, soaked overnight;
   if canned, drained)

¼ cup fresh dill (or 2 tablespoons plus 2 teaspoons dried)

2 tablespoons lemon juice

Place diced eggplant in a perforated pan and sprinkle with the kosher salt. Let stand for 1 hour and pat dry. Preheat olive oil in a large stock pot or kettle. Add the eggplant, onions, garlic, and green bell peppers. Sauté until tender. Add remaining ingredients and cook over medium heat for 40 minutes. Stir occasionally while cooking. Beans should be tender.

SERVES 8

PRESENTATION SUGGESTION: Put chili in a bowl made from a hollowed squash, top with shredded Cheddar and jalapeño jack cheeses, and bake in a preheated 450-degree oven for 10 minutes. Place on a bed of brown rice and serve with corn muffins and Tabasco sauce.

SOUTHWESTERN CHILI

THE SOUTHWEST AND other areas of the country are hopping on the bandwagon, rating chili cook-offs as one of the most popular amateur food festivals. A contestant dresses in urban-Western garb, turns up the Sterno can underneath a pot of meat and tomato sauce, then goes searching for the hottest spices on the planet.

No one knows how old chili recipes are, but their claim to fame was, of course, the Old West. Cattle-driving cowboys moving herds across the plains had no fast-food stops, so chuck wagons were invented. With them came talented cooks, or "cookies," to prepare quick, easy meals on the move.

In a chuck wagon draped in pots, pans, grinders, shovels, and food supplies, the cookie usually preceded the cattle drive to allow time to set up for the cowhands' next stop. Food stocks had to keep for the long treks, so dried beans, dried meats, cans of tomatoes, and the like were the ingredients of the day.

For quick and simple trailside cooking, one-pot meals like chili were a natural. The spices used weren't even close to those of today's nouvelle cook-off cuisine. Chili was basic, hearty and thick, and usually vegetarian. Cattle were far too valuable to slaughter on the trail. However, as palates and food supplies allowed, chili dishes took on new life. Virtually everything was added to bring bulk and variety to the table.

Chili cook-off pros disdain the thought of beans or anything but the finest steak in their chili. This is contrary to the real chili served over a hundred years ago.

Artichokes Stuffed with Gingerbread and Pine Nuts

Heartline Café, Sedona, Arizona

CHEF CHARLES R. CLINE

¼ pound (1 stick) unsalted butter

⅓ cup firmly packed brown sugar

½ cup granulated sugar

¼ cup molasses

1 large egg

1 teaspoon vanilla

1 teaspoon fresh minced ginger

1½ cups all-purpose baking flour

1 teaspoon baking soda

¾ teaspoon ground ginger

½ cup sour cream

¼ cup milk

¼ cup chopped parsley

¼ cup toasted pine nuts

1 teaspoon chopped fresh thyme (or ½ teaspoon dried)

Salt and pepper

20 canned medium artichoke hearts, drained and bottoms
   trimmed flat

Herb sprigs for garnish

Preheat oven to 325 degrees.

In a large bowl, mix butter, sugars, molasses, egg, and vanilla. Add minced ginger, flour, baking soda, and ground ginger. Add sour cream and milk. Mix well with a whisk for about 5 minutes. Pour into a 10-inch

OPPOSITE: *Artichokes Stuffed with Gingerbread and Pine Nuts*

cake pan and bake for 55 minutes. Remove cake from pan when cool and crumble into pieces. Mix in parsley, pine nuts, thyme, salt, and pepper. Stuff this mixture into the artichoke hearts. Place stuffed artichokes on a flat sheet pan and heat in oven for about 10 minutes.

Place the Lemon-Garlic Aïoli (recipe follows) on the bottom of a serving platter, or place 1 tablespoon of the aïoli on each serving plate. Place warmed artichokes on top and garnish with herb sprigs.

SERVES 4

LEMON-GARLIC AÏOLI

6 cloves garlic, peeled
Juice of 2 lemons
3 egg yolks
½ cup olive oil
Salt and pepper

In a food processor, make a paste from the garlic, lemon juice, and egg yolks. Slowly drizzle the olive oil into the paste while the blade is turning. When the mixture has thickened a little, add salt and pepper.

AUTHOR'S NOTE: Yet another very creative blend of flavors, this recipe also works well as an accompaniment to another entrée.

Southwestern Quiche

The Peacock Room, Hassayampa Inn, Prescott, Arizona

CHEF RANDALL J. BONNEVILLE

8 ounces jalapeño jack cheese, shredded

2 green chile peppers, roasted and peeled

2 scallions, diced

4 ounces black olives, sliced

1 ounce sun-dried tomatoes, rehydrated and chopped

1 9-inch deep-dish pic shcll

3 eggs

1 cup milk

1 cup half-and-half

¼ teaspoon salt

¼ teaspoon white pepper

½ teaspoon nutmeg

Preheat oven to 350 degrees.

Place cheese in a medium-size bowl, add green chiles, scallions, black olives, and sun-dried tomatoes, and toss. Put mixture into pie shell. Whip together eggs, milk, half-and-half, salt, pepper, and nutmeg. Pour liquid mixture over cheese mixture until shell is full. Push down the cheese and vegetables so the egg mixture covers all of them. Bake for 35 to 40 minutes or until the custard sets and browns.

SERVES 4

AUTHOR'S NOTE: The egg custard is set when the middle of the quiche is still slightly loose and the sides lightly browned.

Spanish Omelet con Salsa por Ocho Chiles

The Oaks Restaurant, Payson, Arizona

CHEF JACK L. ETTER II

SALSA POR OCHO CHILES

4 large red tomatoes, peeled, seeded, and coarsely chopped

2 large yellow tomatoes, peeled, seeded, and coarsely chopped

1 small green bell pepper, seeded and diced

1 small red bell pepper, seeded and diced

1 Anaheim chile, finely diced

1 ancho chile, finely diced

1 poblano chile, finely diced

3 jalapeño chiles, finely minced

3 serrano chiles, finely minced

3 cayenne chiles, finely minced

1 small white onion, diced

1 small red onion, diced

3 scallions, diced

1 bunch cilantro, coarsely chopped

6 cloves garlic, finely minced

1 tablespoon cumin

1 tablespoon chili powder

2 tablespoons crushed red pepper

1 tablespoon dried oregano

1 tablespoon freshly ground black pepper

Salt to taste

Core and score red and yellow tomatoes and immerse in boiling water for approximately 5 seconds or until the skin begins to loosen. Remove immediately to ice bath and let tomatoes cool. Peel the tomatoes and cut them in half horizontally. Remove the seeds and juice and set them aside. Chop tomatoes coarsely and place them in a sieve. Set tomatoes aside.

Place the bell peppers, chiles, onions, scallions, cilantro, and garlic in a large bowl. Add the tomatoes and remaining spices. Add half of the set-aside tomato juice and seeds. Toss mixture gently and let it set for a few minutes. For a thinner salsa, add more of the juice. Set aside 3 ounces (about ⅓ cup) of salsa for each omelet; chill the rest.

SPANISH OMELET

    1 tablespoon butter
    3 eggs, thoroughly beaten
    2 ounces grated pepper cheese
    3 ounces Salsa por Ocho Chiles, heated
    Guacamole for garnish (optional)
    Sour cream for garnish (optional)
    Fresh fruit for garnish

Melt the butter in a 6- to 8-inch nonstick omelete pan. Add beaten eggs and stir slightly with a nonmetallic spoon. Flip the omelet when top starts to thicken and add half of the pepper cheese and half of a portion of the salsa. Fold the omelete over the filling. Add the remaining salsa and cheese to the top of the omelete and cover. It is done when firm. Serve with guacamole or sour cream, or both, and chilled salsa on the side. Garnish with fruit—grapes, strawberries, and pineapple are especially delicious with this omelet.

SERVES 2

AUTHOR'S NOTE: This recipe yields enough salsa for 6 to 8 servings and will keep for a week. The salsa won the "Southwest Salsa Challenge" in 1986.

ZUCCHINI

Z UCCHINIS ARE RESILIENT summer squash, coming from the same family as pattypans and chayote. They are so easily obtainable you will find them in many traditional Southwestern dishes, including vegetarian. They have thinner skin than their winter squash cousins and are eaten before their rinds harden. Ideally, they should be picked when 3 to 6 inches in length. At this size, they are tender and sweet.

Pan-fried, steamed, boiled, baked, and grilled zucchini does not have an overbearing flavor.

◇ Zucchini is so versatile it can be used in almost any recipe calling for eggplant or cucumber. However, larger sizes should be peeled before substituting.

◇ Steaming is simple. Cut zucchini into small pieces. Steam suspended in a pot of boiling water until tender. This can vary from 5 to 10 minutes, depending on how thickly the pieces are cut. Flavor with butter, white pepper, and a touch of Parmesan cheese.

◇ Baking zucchini requires little effort. Cut into strips, paint with olive oil, and bake, uncovered, for 20 to 30 minutes. Use flavorings of your choice.

◇ If cooked too long, zucchini gets mushy. Save it and purée for soups.

◇ Zucchini can be frozen and used later as a filler in spaghetti sauces, breads, and quiches. Preparation is simple. Peel the skin, remove the seeds, then grate. Next, cook the grated zucchini in butter on high heat (a wok is perfect). Spread in a pan to cool and then freeze every-thing, includ ing the pan. Freeze until hard, then remove from pan and package for storage. Thaw and drain before using.

Grilled Vegetable Salad

Murphy's Restaurant, Prescott, Arizona

CHEF DAVE VILLA

¼ cup olive oil

2   cloves garlic, minced

1   tablespoon minced fresh thyme, (or substitute basil or parsley)

Fresh cracked black pepper

3   pounds vegetables of your choice (such as button mushrooms, any squash, bell peppers, pearl onions, or broccoli)

4   wooden skewers, soaked in water for about 20 minutes

4   cups mixed salad greens

½ cup julienned red onion

1   medium carrot, julienned

1   cup julienned jicama

Champagne Vinaigrette dressing (recipe follows)

8   tablespoons crumbled feta cheese

8   tablespoons pepitas

8   tomato wedges for garnish

Prepare barbecue grill or broiler. In a large bowl, combine olive oil, garlic, thyme, and pepper. Toss vegetables in mixture. Skewer vegetables, beginning and ending with mushrooms and alternating others. Grill or broil until tender.

In another large bowl, toss greens, onion, carrot, and jicama with dressing to coat. Divide among 4 chilled plates. Sprinkle 2 tablespoons crumbled feta cheese and 2 tablespoons pepitas over each plate of salad. Lay a skewer of vegetables on top of each salad and garnish with tomato wedges.

CHAMPAGNE VINAIGRETTE

½ cup passionfruit syrup

⅓ cup champagne vinegar

2 tablespoons red wine vinegar

1 teaspoon finely chopped shallot or red onion

2 tablespoons chopped fresh cilantro

½ cup canola, soybean, or sunflower oil

Place all ingredients in a bowl and whisk thoroughly. Rewhisk before using.

AUTHOR'S NOTE: The selection of vegetables should include your favorites plus a few you have not tried. Cut vegetables to a comfortable size (try 2 inches x 2 inches) so they can be easily handled. Vary the sizes for a delightful visual presentation.

To substitute for passionfruit, use ½ cup orange juice concentrate and 1 tablespoon grenadine. Blend well.

SERVES 4

Enchantment of the Spring Forest and Garden

Janos, Tucson, Arizona

CHEF JANOS

1 tablespoon Basil Oil (recipe follows)

1 cup fresh, cleaned green beans, lightly blanched

12 ounces fresh baby carrots, lightly blanched

12 ounces baby squash pieces (your choice), lightly blanched

24 ounces asparagus

12 ounces fresh, cleaned portabello, chanterelle, shiitake, oyster, or other mushrooms

VINEGAR

A BOTTLE OF WINE left to the air gathers yeast and ferments; for better or worse, vinegar results. When discovered a few millennia ago, vinegar was used to flavor mixes of sweet and sour foods and as a dip for breads, a beverage for soldiers, and a medicine for a whole array of ailments.

Centuries ago, cooks were extremely creative with their vinegars, flavoring them with dates, cloves, mustard, truffles, and so on. Since it was popular to pour the strongly flavored liquid over a dinner meal to disguise spoiled foods, it is not hard to understand why palates of our ancestors were a bit more tolerant than today's lively taste buds. Vinegars became so popular they even had containers designated especially to hold them. Antique hounds will recognize the little silver boxes called "vinaigrettes." Seventeenth-century upper crust carried them to hold to their noses to mask vile city smells.

Making vinegar is more complex than making wine. It requires one to make respectable wine first and, assuming it is palatable, to make vinegar from the wine. This double fermentation process is risky. Good vinegar requires good wine and, unfortunately, most of today's vinegars are made from some winemakers' second pressings, or worse.

But there is hope. A new trend—Italian aceto balsamico vinegar—is making good headway. It is a centuries-old process for making a high-quality vinegar. True aceto balsamico vinegar (more commonly called "balsamic") is expensive because it takes many grapes to develop and many years to age properly. However, its current popularity means chefs are taking vinegars seriously.

1 cup snow peas

1 tablespoon chopped fresh garlic

1 tablespoon chopped fresh basil (or 1 teaspoon dried)

1 tablespoon aged balsamic vinegar

1 teaspoon Sun-Dried Tomato Oil (recipe follows)

Salt and pepper to taste

Grated Parmesan cheese for garnish

Squirt some basil oil into a hot sauté pan and add the green beans, carrots, squash, and asparagus. Sauté for about 1 minute before adding the mushrooms, snow peas, and garlic. Squirt with some more basil oil for flavor, tossing the ingredients in the pan. Sauté another minute or so, then sprinkle the chopped basil over the vegetables. Divide among four individual plates and drizzle with a little balsamic vinegar and tomato oil. Season to taste with salt and pepper and garnish with Parmesan.

SERVES 4

BASIL OIL

½ cup fresh basil

Boiling water

Ice water

1 cup olive oil

Blanch the basil in the boiling water for about 30 seconds, then remove and plunge in the iced water to set the color of the basil. Dry the basil and purée it with the olive oil. Let the oil steep as is in a squirt bottle, or strain the oil before pouring it into the squirt bottle.

SUN-DRIED TOMATO OIL

1 cup olive oil

½ cup sun-dried tomatoes

Purée the tomatoes with the olive oil and let steep overnight or longer. Strain and pour into a squirt bottle.

Vegetable Paella

The Wigwam Resort,
Litchfield Park, Arizona

CHEF JON HILL

1 cup olive oil

2 leeks, white part only, chopped

4 onions, chopped

4 cloves garlic, chopped

4 small tomatoes, peeled, seeded, and chopped

8 fresh artichoke hearts

4 red bell peppers, roasted, peeled, and julienned

2 cups cauliflower florets

½ pound shelled green peas

5 cups vegetable stock (about three 13¾-ounce cans)

Salt and pepper to taste

4 teaspoons chopped fresh cilantro

1 pound short grain rice

In a casserole (preferably an earthenware casserole) over low heat, heat the oil. Add half of the leeks, onions, garlic, and tomatoes. Cook for 2 minutes. Add artichoke hearts, bell peppers, cauliflower, and peas. Add half of the vegetable stock and cook on low heat for 10 minutes; season with salt and pepper. Add the remainder of the leeks, onions, tomatoes, garlic, all the cilantro, the rice, and the rest of the stock and blend. Cook for another 20 minutes or so until rice is done. Add more stock if needed.

SERVES 6 TO 8

AUTHOR'S NOTE: This paella is very easy to assemble. The flavors of the fresh vegetables are so pronounced even nonvegetarians will rave. See "Vegetable Stocks," pages 124 to 125, for more information on creating one.

If fresh artichoke hearts are not available, use canned hearts, and rinse.

Poblano Chiles Stuffed with Pasta, Olives, and Sun-Dried Tomatoes

Café Terra Cotta, Scottsdale, Arizona

MATTHEW LASH

2 cups uncooked orzo pasta

1 cup sliced black olives

1 cup sliced sun-dried tomatoes

2 cloves garlic, minced

2 tablespoons chopped fresh parsley

1 teaspoon freshly ground black pepper

2 tablespoons capers, drained

1 cup shredded skim milk (or part skim) mozzarella

12 large poblano chiles, roasted and peeled with stems intact, sliced lengthwise on one side only, and seeded

2 teaspoons olive oil

Preheat oven to 350 degrees.

Cook the orzo in boiling salted water for 4 to 5 minutes. Drain and cool. Mix together the orzo, olives, sun-dried tomatoes, garlic, parsley, pepper, capers, and mozzarella. Divide mixture into 12 equal portions and spoon into poblanos. Carefully fold one edge of the chile over the other and place seam side down on a lightly oiled baking sheet. Bake for 20 to 30 minutes. Serve immediately.

SERVES 4 TO 6

AUTHOR'S NOTE: Café Terra Cotta serves this with jicama salad, black beans, and warm flour tortillas for a flavorful Southwestern main course.

OPPOSITE: *Vegetable Paella (recipe page 73)*

NATIVE AMERICAN INFLUENCE

M UCH OF OUR daily eating is a direct result of Native American cultivation and harvesting, especially in the Southwest. Pumpkins, tomatoes, avocados, sweet potatoes, white potatoes, peppers, and, of course, corn are a few major contributions. And much of what is thought of as Mexican food is really a Native American innovation. For example, refried beans, tamales, and enchiladas were created by Southwestern tribes long before the arrival of the Spaniards.

Native American cuisine has mingled with Southwestern regional foods so much that it may be hard to define. Sample dishes include wild fowl eggs scrambled in wild rice, puréed piñon cakes, cactus salad with crushed dried peppers, and green chile stew.

Meats and vegetables can be prepared indoors or out. First a modest hole is dug, then lined with rocks and brush, and set on fire. When the rocks are hot, a fresh buffalo or deer skin is laid over the rocks, then meat or vegetables are placed on it. Then the whole dinner is buried.

Southwestern tribes bake in *hornos,* beehive-shaped, compact adobe ovens. The hard-packed, sunbaked clay acts as an insulator for the tremendous heat generated by brush gathered to build the fire. After the oven is brought to temperature, embers are brushed out and bread is put in to bake. The door is covered with a sheepskin flap to hold in radiant heat. A talented hand knows just when the bread is done. The *hornos* produce thick-crusted breads as good as any.

Santa Fe Vegetarian Harvest Platter with Grilled Vegetables, Heirloom Beans, Roasted Tomato Salsa, and Tree Fruit Tamales

La Casa Sena Restaurant and Cantina, Santa Fe, New Mexico

CHEF KELLY ROGERS

GRILLED VEGETABLES

1 large onion
1 ear sweet corn, cooked
1 acorn squash, partially roasted
1 potato, cleaned and cooked
2 New Mexican green chiles, split and seeded
Balsamic vinegar
Olive oil
Salt and pepper to taste
4 flour tortillas

Heat a grill.

Making sure *not* to cut into the bottom connecting part of the onion, make deep incisions to separate it into four barely connected quarters. Cut the corn, squash, and potato into 4 equal pieces each. Toss the vegetables, including the chiles, in a splash of balsamic vinegar, olive oil, and salt and pepper.

Grill until char marks appear on the surfaces of the vegetables. When taking them off the grill, lay them out without stacking them and let cool on a sheet pan.

To serve, grill a flour tortilla and place it on a plate. Top with the

Heirloom Beans (recipe follows). Spoon the Roasted Tomato Salsa (recipe follows) over the beans. Arrange the vegetables around the plate and drizzle with balsamic vinegar and olive oil. Place the steamed Tree Fruit Tamale (recipe follows) on top with the husk peeled back. Repeat for each serving.

SERVES 4

HEIRLOOM BEANS

2 cups of a variety of dried beans
1 onion, chopped
4 cloves garlic, minced
1 jalapeño, seeded and diced

Soak the beans in water overnight. Drain, add fresh water just to cover. Add onion, garlic, and jalapeño and bring to a boil. Cover and simmer until beans are soft.

ROASTED TOMATO SALSA

4 plum tomatoes
1 serrano chile, minced
1 red onion, diced into ¼-inch cubes
2 cloves garlic, finely diced
Salt and pepper to taste
2 tablespoons vegetable oil
1 teaspoon ground cumin, toasted
1 teaspoon lime juice
2 tablespoons chopped cilantro
⅛ cup dark beer

Preheat oven to 400 degrees.
Toss tomatoes, serrano chile, onion, garlic, salt, and pepper in oil and

roast for 20 to 30 minutes until vegetables are soft and browned. Cool, dice tomatoes, and toss vegetables with cumin, lime juice, cilantro, and beer.

TREE FRUIT TAMALES

1 apple, peeled, cored, and diced into ¼-inch pieces

1 pear, peeled, cored, and diced into ¼-inch pieces

2 tablespoons butter

1 teaspoon cinnamon

Salt to taste

¼ cup vegetable shortening

1 cup masa harina

¼ teaspoon baking powder

½ cup warm water

pinch of salt

Corn husks or plastic wrap

Sauté the apple and pear in butter for about 5 minutes. Add cinnamon and salt to taste. (The tamale fruit filling will cook more when steamed in the masa.)

Whip the shortening until fluffy. Add masa harina, baking powder, water, and salt. Blend with a large spoon, mixing the masa until it is soft and pliable. Spread the masa mixture ¼-inch thick on the centers of the corn husks, or plastic wrap, in a 3 x 4-inch area. Spoon about 1 tablespoon of the fruit filling onto the center of the masa. Fold each husk or piece of plastic over the masa and close both ends to seal the tamale. Wrap the tamales together in a wet cloth and place the package in a sealed steamer for 1 hour. If you don't have a steamer, wrap the towel in foil and bake the package in a preheated 350-degree oven for 1 hour.

AUTHOR'S NOTE: The chef says this dish is very symbolic of a fall harvest in New Mexico. It is a seasonal dish with all the color one can imagine. However, if you make this out of season, just substitute whatever fresh vegetables are available for "harvest vegetables."

TOMATOES

I T IS SPECULATED that tomatoes made their first appearance as weeds in maize and bean fields in what is now Mexico. The natives found them easy to cultivate and eventually used them with many other foods. When the New World "visitors" came knocking, they didn't trust the strange fruit and thought it poisonous. Whether as a joke, or as a curiosity, the explorers sent seeds home to Spain. History does not tell of the curious transformation, but tomato popularity skyrocketed when identified as a powerful aphrodisiac, "love apples."

One of the tomato's more notable achievements was its use as one of the first products successfully canned and distributed in this country. By the late 1800s canned tomatoes were extremely popular, especially in the Southwest. Chuckwagon and range cooks found them easy to mix and useful to vary a tiresome menu. For cowboys the liquid served as a welcome respite from the dry Western heat. Cowpokes often carried extra cans in their saddlebags to refresh themselves throughout the day.

From these unlikely roots, tomatoes spread as a reliable world crop. It's possible to do almost anything with them: They are a predictable base for many creations. Some interesting tomato facts:

> Tomatoes are loaded with vitamins A and C.

> Vine-ripened tomatoes always beat those picked green and ripened on the windowsill.

> Tomatoes freeze very poorly; the best way is to freeze them as a sauce.

- Do not preslice tomatoes and store. They are best if prepared and served immediately.

- Once opened, canned tomatoes last about ten days refrigerated. Store in plastic or glass, not in the original can.

- If adding fresh tomatoes to a dish, reduce other liquids. Tomatoes contain a lot of water.

To make a good sauce base, add seasonings like basil, thyme, garlic, and onion, plus a bit of red wine, to properly prepared tomatoes. You'll have the sauce of your dreams. To prepare tomatoes:

1. First, peel the tomatoes in one of three ways:

   - Dip in boiling water for 30 seconds or so and then plunge into cold water. The skin will peel right off.

   - Impale the tomato with a fork and hold it over a flame until the skin blisters. Dip it into cold water and the cracked skin will slip off.

   - Peel very ripe tomatoes by rubbing them firmly with the back of a knife and pulling the skin clear.

2. Cut around the stem and pull out the tough part. Cut into chunks and simmer, usually 20 minutes or more, in a nonstick pot until the desired thickness is reached.

Hours on the stove with fresh spices added makes a sauce from heaven. However, if you prefer a speedy solution, thicken the sauce with bread crumbs or cornstarch. To reduce the acid flavor of the stewed tomatoes, add a couple tablespoons of sugar while simmering.

Wild Mushroom Ragout with Green Chile-Spiked Polenta

The Tack Room, Tucson, Arizona

CHEF RODNEY L. TIMM

WILD MUSHROOM RAGOUT

- 2 tablespoons olive oil
- 4 tablespoons unsalted butter
- ½ cup chopped shallots
- 4 cloves garlic, minced
- 1 pound fresh wild mushrooms (such as oyster or shiitake), cut into bite-size pieces
- 1 cup red wine
- 1 tablespoon cornstarch
- 2 tablespoons water
- 2 tablespoons chopped fresh herbs (basil, oregano, thyme, or sage)
- Salt and pepper to taste

Heat oil and butter in a medium-size pan until butter is melted. Sauté shallots and garlic until translucent. Add mushrooms and sauté until softened. Deglaze pan with red wine and simmer 10 minutes.

Dissolve cornstarch in small amount of water and stir into ragout. Add herbs and season to taste. Serve over Green Chile–Spiked Polenta (recipe follows).

GREEN CHILE–SPIKED POLENTA

1 tablespoon olive oil

½ cup chopped white onion

¼ cup peeled, seeded, and diced Anaheim or poblano chiles

3 cups water or vegetable stock

1½ cups cornmeal

¼ cup grated Parmesan cheese

Salt and pepper to taste

Heat oil and sauté onion. Add green chiles. Stir in water or stock and bring to a boil. Whisk in cornmeal slowly to avoid lumps. Cook slowly until thickened, stirring constantly until polenta pulls away from side of pan. Stir in cheese and salt and pepper to taste. Spread out ½-inch thick on 8 x 8-inch baking sheet and cool. Cut into pieces, brush with olive oil, and grill until heated thoroughly. Top with Wild Mushroom Ragout.

SERVES 2 TO 4

AUTHOR'S NOTE: See "deglazing" in the glossary for more information about this process. Remember that polenta must be cooked slowly to ensure the proper consistency. If cooked too quickly, the ground corn will not expand.

Barbecue Tofu and Eggplant Wrap with Mixed Greens

Golden Swan, Hyatt Regency, Scottsdale, Arizona

CHEF ANTON BRUNBAUER

½ cup plus 3 tablespoons olive oil

2½ cups barbecue sauce (your choice)

¼ cup fresh lemon juice

1   tablespoon chopped garlic
1   tablespoon chopped oregano
1   tablespoon chopped basil
18 ounces tofu, drained and cut into twelve slices
1   medium eggplant, cut into twelve ¼-inch slices
3   tablespoons olive oil
4   (12-inch) jalapeño-cilantro tortillas, warmed
3   medium carrots, peeled and julienned
1   medium jicama, peeled and julienned
1   medium cucumber, seeded and julienned

In a medium-size bowl, prepare the marinade by combining ½ cup of the olive oil, ½ cup of the barbecue sauce, lemon juice, garlic, oregano, and basil.

Marinate tofu and eggplant in barbecue sauce mixture for at least an hour and no longer than overnight.

In a large skillet over medium heat, add 3 tablespoons of olive oil and sauté tofu and eggplant for 3 to 4 minutes on each side. Divide the remaining barbecue sauce among 4 warmed tortillas, adding 3 slices of tofu, 3 slices of eggplant, and ¼ of the julienned carrots, jicama, and cucumber to each tortilla. Roll the tortillas and cut each into 3 slices. Place on plates and serve with mixed greens.

SERVES 4

AUTHOR'S NOTE: Plain or whole wheat tortillas can be substituted for jalapeño-cilantro tortillas. Sprigs of fresh cilantro can be added if desired.

To julienne carrots, jicama, and cucumber, slice thinly into strips.

Vegetarian Burrito with Green Chile Sauce

Carlsbad Tavern, Scottsdale, Arizona

CHEF JAMES H. SMITH, JR.

VEGETARIAN BURRITO

- 2 tablespoons vegetable oil
- 1 tablespoon minced garlic
- 1 cup broccoli florets
- 1 cup julienned red onion
- 2 cups seeded and julienned red bell peppers
- 2 cups seeded and julienned green bell peppers
- 2 jalapeños, diced (the larger the dice, the hotter the taste)
- 2 cups julienned zucchini (approximately ⅛ x ⅛ x 2 inches)
- 2 cups julienned yellow squash
- 1 cup diced plum tomatoes

Salt and pepper to taste

- 8 (10-inch) flour tortillas
- 4 cups shredded Monterey jack cheese

Green Chile Sauce (recipe follows)

Lettuce for garnish

Sour cream for garnish

Salsa for garnish

Preheat oven to 325 degrees.

Heat a large skillet, add the vegetable oil, then sauté garlic, broccoli, onion, bell peppers, and jalapeños. Toss frequently until tender. Stir in zucchini and yellow squash and cook until crisp yet tender, about 3 to 4 minutes. Add tomatoes and cook 1 or 2 minutes more. Season with salt and pepper.

Warm the flour tortillas (a cold burrito may tear when rolled). Spoon about 1 cup of sautéed vegetables and ¼ cup shredded cheese in center of tortilla. Fold bottom end of tortilla up about 1 inch over the vegetables. Overlap left and right flaps, then roll into a cylinder, placing the seam side down. Place burritos on an oven-safe platter or cookie sheet.

Cover burritos with Green Chile Sauce and sprinkle with Monterey jack cheese. Bake for 8 to 10 minutes or until cheese melts. Garnish with lettuce, sour cream, and salsa. Serve with rice and beans.

SERVES 8

GREEN CHILE SAUCE

3½ pounds mild to hot green chiles, roasted, peeled and diced
1 pound plum tomatoes, diced
1 pound yellow onions, diced
½ tablespoon minced garlic
1½ tablespoons coarse salt
½ tablespoon cracked black pepper
1 tablespoon dried oregano
5 cups water, plus ¼ cup cool water
2 tablespoons cornstarch

In a 4-quart pot, combine chiles, tomatoes, onions, garlic, salt, pepper, oregano, and 5 cups of the water. Bring to a boil, then lower heat to a simmer. Cook, uncovered, for 1 to 1½ hours. Then turn the heat up until the sauce comes to a very slow boil.

Mix together cornstarch and ¼ cup cool water to form a slurry. Turn the heat off under the sauce and immediately and slowly add the slurry while stirring rapidly. (Failure to turn off heat may result in the cornstarch scorching the pan.)

You should have a smooth, pourable sauce that will stay on top of your burritos while some of it runs down the sides onto the plate—perfect for sopping up with tortillas or sopapillas, a truly wonderful New Mexican tradition.

OPPOSITE: *Vegetarian Burrito with Green Chili Sauce (recipe page 85)*

YIELDS 2½ QUARTS

AUTHOR'S NOTE: If the cornstarch fails to thicken the sauce to your liking, there are two options: Continue to simmer the sauce to cook it down or add an additional tablespoon of cornstarch.

~~~~~~~~~~~~~

Lentil Cakes with Nopalito and Arizona Apples Relish

Razz's Restaurant and Bar, Scottsdale, Arizona

CHEF ERASMO "RAZZ" KAMNITZER

LENTIL CAKES

4 cups water
1 cup red and/or yellow lentils
1 cup green lentils
1 cup diced mixed bell peppers (red, yellow, and green)
¼ cup diced scallions
¼ cup diced mixed onions (red, yellow, and white)
2 eggs or 5 ounces tofu
1 cup bread crumbs
¼ cup chopped chives
¼ cup finely diced carrots
¼ cup finely diced celery
Salt and pepper to taste
Oil for frying (approximately ¼-inch in a large sauté pan)

In enough water to cover (about 2 cups for each 1 cup of lentils), cook red and green lentils separately until tender, about 15 minutes for the red and 25 minutes for the green. Drain and pat dry. Purée red

88 ◇ VEGETARIAN SOUTHWEST

lentils, then stir in whole green lentils, peppers, scallions, onions, eggs (or tofu), bread crumbs, chives, carrots, celery, and salt and pepper to taste. Divide into 24 equal portions and form into individual cakes.

In a large sauté pan, heat oil and pan fry the cakes until golden brown. Serve with Nopalito Cactus and Arizona Apples Relish (recipe follows) on the side or on the cakes.

SERVES 4 TO 6

NOPALITO CACTUS AND ARIZONA APPLES RELISH

1 nopalito pad, thorns and needles removed, diced small (approximately ½ cup)

½ cup peeled and diced apples

½ cup diced mixed peppers (sweet and hot)

½ cup peeled mixed citrus segments (orange, grapefruit, lime)

½ cup diced tomatoes

1 tablespoon chopped fresh chives

3 tablespoons chopped fresh cilantro

2 tablespoons diced onion

Juice of 2 limes

2 tablespoons olive oil

Salt and pepper to taste

1 teaspoon chopped elephant garlic

In a large mixing bowl, combine all ingredients and season to taste.

AUTHOR'S NOTE: This dish is simple to blend and cook, has a delightful flavor, and makes a colorful presentation.

SPICING UP
SOUTHWESTERN DISHES

As in much of the world, spice availability in the United States is highly regionalized. Factors like transportation and a spice's ability to grow in a given area determine its popularity. The delicate spicing of many dishes developed over many centuries by European chefs traveled with immigrants to the Americas. However, use in the Southwest of many of these well-known foods and spices was virtually impossible due to arid conditions and lack of a major transportation network. The Southwest missed out compared to the rest of the growing nation.

To compensate, spices from this region became very distinctive. The strong Native American and Mexican influences provided dried chiles, cactus, and other indigenous plants. Most of these remain in use today in Southwestern cuisine. Accents like cilantro also add valuable flavoring to many regional dishes.

Which brings us to the care and handling of Southwestern spices. Here are a few hints to help keep spices at their peak:

> Buy spices as fresh as possible, pulling the jars from the back of the display to get those likely to be most recently shelved. Never purchase a spice with dust on its container.

> Purchase spices in screw-top jars. These retard invasion of air, which accelerates loss of freshness.

> Taste test spices in the store if possible. If not, look for

spices that are brightly and consistently colored throughout the container. Fading is usually a sign of flavor loss.

> It is not a good idea to store spices above the stove. Moisture and heat are a spice's two worst enemies. The cooler and drier the storage area, the longer the spice will maintain its fragrance.

> Ground spices keep for about one year. After that you are really testing their endurance and it's safer to throw them out.

> To tell if a spice has lots its punch, rub a pinch between your fingers and smell it. If the aroma is insignificant, the spice will do little for your food.

> A good way to maximize spice potential is to soak it in some kind of liquid—such as water, wine, or oil—that can be incorporated into the recipe. Just mix in the spice and let the infused liquid sit for up to one hour prior to use.

Vegetable Terrine with Tomato-Chile Coulis

House of Tricks, Tempe, Arizona

CHEF HECTOR ALBARRAN

VEGETABLE TERRINE

Olive oil as needed

1 bunch napa cabbage, separated and blanched

6 large portabello mushrooms, roasted

6 yellow bell peppers, roasted

1 large eggplant, roasted

Salt and pepper to taste

Polenta (recipe follows)

Tomato-Chile Coulis (recipe follows)

Rub the inside of a large metal pâté mold with olive oil. Line the inside of the mold with cabbage leaves, allowing approximately 2 inches to overhang on all sides. Slice the roasted mushrooms, bell peppers, and eggplant to fit neatly into the mold and layer them alternately in the mold, sprinkling lightly with salt and pepper. Repeat until 2 or 3 layers of each vegetable are made. Pour the soft polenta (recipe follows) into the mold until it almost reaches the top. Fold the overhanging cabbage leaves in over the polenta to cover completely. Chill until the polenta sets.

Preheat oven to 300 degrees. Cover mold with foil and bake for 20 to 25 minutes, or until internal temperature reaches 125 degrees.

Carefully unmold the terrine and slice for presentation. Spoon warm tomato coulis onto serving plates and top with sliced terrine.

SERVES 4

OPPOSITE: *Vegetable Terrine with Tomato-Chile Coulis*

POLENTA

1 cup cornmeal

3 cups milk

1/4 cup Parmesan, shredded

1 tablespoon butter

fresh herbs as desired

In a saucepan, bring milk and butter to a boil. Turn off heat and whisk in the cornmeal until lumps are gone. Whisk in Parmesan and desired herbs. Cover and let sit 8 minutes.

TOMATO-CHILE COULIS

1 to 2 tablespoons olive oil

1 clove garlic, minced

½ chipotle chile, minced

3 fresh tomatoes, diced

Salt and pepper to taste

Sauté garlic and chipotle in a little olive oil. Add tomatoes and cook until they are completely soft. Purée and season to taste with salt and pepper. Strain. Keep warm.

AUTHOR'S NOTE: If a pâté mold is not in your inventory, try a springform pan.

Stuffed Anaheim Chiles

The Ranchers Club of New Mexico, Albuquerque Hilton, Albuquerque, New Mexico

CHEF RICHARD C. PERALES

1 tablespoon light butter

¼ cup minced red onion

¼ cup whole kernel corn

3 ounces tofu, diced

1 teaspoon chopped fresh cilantro

2 ounces Monterey jack cheese, shredded

2 medium Anaheim chiles, roasted, peeled, and seeded

1 cup black beans (any recipe)

¼ cup sour cream for garnish

¼ cup salsa for garnish

¼ cup chopped scallions for garnish

In a medium-size pan over medium heat, melt butter and sauté onion, corn, and tofu for 5 minutes. Add cilantro and cheese and mix thoroughly. (The cheese should melt just enough to make the stuffing process easier.) Let the mixture cool for 5 minutes, then divide it equally. Gently stuff half of the mixture into each roasted chile. Strain all excess liquid from beans and pour the black beans equally over two large dinner plates. Lay one stuffed chile in the center of each plate. Garnish with sour cream, salsa, and scallions.

SERVES 2

AUTHOR'S NOTE: For the black beans, use a recipe in this book or purchase a canned preparation.

Corn Pappardelle with Fresh Roasted Corn and Poblano Chile Sauce

Café de las Placitas, Placitas, New Mexico

CHEF MATHEW BESSE-BREWER

CORN PAPPARDELLE

Equal amounts whole eggs, masa harina, semolina flour, and all-purpose flour to make a firm dough.

Beat eggs lightly and mix in enough masa harina and semolina flour to form a firm dough. Roll the dough very thin and cut into 1-inch x 12-inch strips. Blanch in hot water and chill.

SERVES 4

FRESH ROASTED CORN AND POBLANO CHILE SAUCE

¼ cup olive oil

2 tablespoons chopped garlic

1 tablespoon chopped shallot

2 cups vegetable stock

½ cup roasted, seeded, and chopped poblano chile

2 cups roasted fresh corn

1 tablespoon crushed, toasted cumin seed

2 cups chopped fresh tomatoes

2 tablespoons soft butter

2 tablespoons chopped cilantro

Juice of 1 lime

Salt and pepper to taste

½ cup toasted pine nuts for garnish

1 cup grated Romano cheese for garnish

In medium to large pan, heat oil over medium heat. Sauté garlic and shallot and add enough vegetable stock to prevent excessive browning. Add chile, corn, cumin, tomatoes and remaining stock. Reduce, uncovered, by half. Turn off heat and add butter, cilantro, and lime juice, stirring frequently until butter melts. Adjust seasonings with salt and pepper.

Reheat pappardelle pasta in water and strain. Toss pasta with sauce and serve. Garnish with pine nuts and Romano cheese.

AUTHOR'S NOTE: If homemade pasta is too much work, purchase fresh wide egg noodles. Dried, packaged fettuccine will also work, but it lacks the delicious corn flavor. For roasted corn, you may broil canned (drained) or frozen corn in an oven until firm.

~~~~~~~

Grilled Vegetable Casserole

The Ranchers Club of Arizona, Tucson, Arizona

CHEF ROBERT KOWALSKE

Parchment paper

6 to 8 individual ovenproof casserole dishes

Nonstick vegetable oil spray

6 new red potatoes, sliced ¼-inch thick and blanched

Salt and pepper to taste

1 large yellow squash, thinly sliced and grilled or broiled

1 bunch spinach, steamed

2 medium red onions, julienned and caramelized

1 tablespoon chopped garlic

CORN

THE MOST POPULAR food in the Southwest is corn. It has always permeated virtually every aspect of Native American life. Not only was it a dietary staple, but every available part has been used for a variety of purposes. The black powdery fungus—chapetes, or "corn smut"—found on corn stalks was used for medicinal purposes. Leftover corn was fermented by Apache and Chiricahua tribes and made into a popular alcoholic beverage called "Tula-pah." Traditionally, Native Americans attached ceremony to every stage of corn growth. Many tribes chanted during planting of the "Blessed Daughter," and songs were sung during its gathering.

Also termed "maize" in many references, corn is America's contribution to the world's great grains. Early explorers of the Americas found corn so sweet and nutritious that it was among the first seeds of any plant carried back to Europe.

A member of the grass family, modern corn is usually harvested from May through September. Some types grow well into December but not the sweet variety that is most popular.

Selection of fresh corn is easy. Look for bright-green husks and slightly browned silk at the end of the husks. Ideally, the corn will lie in neat rows on the cob and the kernels will be firm but milky when pierced.

Use corn as soon as possible. It does not keep well on the cob. Of course, it is available year-round frozen or canned.

For recipes, use frozen corn as you would fresh. Drain canned corn well before use and add the packing water to your vegetable stock.

1 tablespoon chopped fresh oregano (or 1 teaspoon dried)

1 tablespoon chopped fresh thyme (or 1 teaspoon dried)

20 medium shiitake mushroom caps, grilled or broiled

1 large zucchini, thinly sliced and grilled or broiled

1 medium butternut squash, peeled, thinly sliced, and grilled or broiled

4 medium red chile peppers, roasted, seeded, and peeled

1 (12-ounce) box quinoa, cooked according to package instructions

Cut circles of parchment paper that will fit into the bottoms of each casserole dish. Set parchment aside. Spray the bottoms and insides of each dish generously with nonstick spray. Lay the parchment circles into the dishes and spray with nonstick spray again.

Preheat oven to 325 degrees.

Layer the potatoes equally into each dish, overlapping slices to form a spiral. As you layer, sprinkle each vegetable with a little salt and pepper. Next, layer the yellow squash. Then add a layer of spinach, then a combination of the caramelized onion, garlic, oregano, and thyme, and then the mushrooms. Next, layer the zucchini, then the butternut squash, then the chiles. Add the cooked quinoa last and pat it down.

Place casseroles in a baking pan, cover with foil, and bake for 1 hour. To serve, unmold each casserole dish by placing a serving plate on top, turning it over to release the contents, and removing any parchment paper that adheres.

SERVES 6 TO 8

AUTHOR'S NOTE: See "Roasting Chiles," page 10, for more information about preparing chile peppers.

The parchment paper is necessary and will keep the well-browned potatoes from sticking to the casserole dish when turned over. This is a beautiful presentation.

Calabacitas and Blue Corn Tortilla Cazuela with Pumpkin Seed Mole

Doc Martin's at the Taos Inn, Taos, New Mexico

PATRICK LAMBERT

CALABACITAS AND BLUE CORN TORTILLA CAZUELA

1 cup vegetable broth

1 cup diced yellow squash

1 cup diced zucchini

1 cup frozen corn

2 cups diced white onion

8 fresh Anaheim chiles, seeded and peeled, or 1½ cups frozen green chiles

1 cup diced red bell pepper

1 cup diced green bell pepper

2 tablespoons ground coriander

¼ cup minced garlic

2 tablespoons fresh oregano (or 2 teaspoons dried)

1 tablespoon ground cumin

Salt to taste

2 tablespoons olive oil

18 to 24 blue or white corn tortillas

Pumpkin Seed Mole (recipe follows)

1 pound Monterey jack cheese, shredded

1 pound Cheddar cheese, shredded

OPPOSITE: *Calabacitas and Blue Corn Tortilla Cazuela with Pumpkin Seed Mole*

In a large pan, heat vegetable broth and add yellow squash, zucchini, corn, onion, chiles, bell peppers, coriander, garlic, oregano, and cumin. Cook until vegetables are tender, adding salt to taste. Do not overcook. Set aside.

Heat a small amount of olive oil in a medium saucepan on medium heat and fry tortillas until they are soft. Place a layer of tortillas on the bottom of a 4-quart casserole dish.

Preheat oven to 350 degrees.

Spread Pumpkin Seed Mole, then half the vegetable mixture (calabacitas) and a third each of the cheeses, followed by the rest of the vegetables, a third more of each of the cheeses, and a layer of tortillas covered with the remaining cheese. Bake, covered, until cheese is melted, about 45 minutes.

SERVES 8

PUMPKIN SEED MOLE

- 2 cups shelled pumpkin seeds
- 2 cups chopped white onion
- 2 tablespoons vegetable oil
- 2½ cups frozen green chiles (or 10 Anaheims), seeded and sliced
- ½ cup vegetable broth
- ½ cup white wine
- 1 tablespoon ground cumin
- Salt to taste
- ½ bunch cilantro, chopped

Preheat oven to 350 degrees.

Roast the pumpkin seeds in a single layer on a cookie sheet until light brown. Sauté the onion in the oil and add the green chiles, broth, wine, cumin, and salt to taste. Continue cooking for another 15 minutes and allow to cool. Purée the onion-chile mixture with the pumpkin seeds and cilantro.

TORTILLAS

As in many other countries with a blend of cultures, the food of the Southwest is highly regionalized, meaning the same dishes are dramatically different throughout the area. In each of the Southwest regions, basic ingredients include a tortilla, a sauce, and a filling, but the tortillas may be folded, stacked, or rolled. They may be baked or fried. They may be filled with a wide variety of ingredients.

In Mexico, most tortilla dishes are served immediately after preparation. Here in the Southwest, they are usually baked and topped with sauce. There is no "correct" method other than discovering what you enjoy and doing it.

The basic step in most meal preparations includes frying the tortilla. Take a bit of oil and heat it, place the tortilla in the hot oil for a few seconds, and turn. The tortilla will blister and become limp. If folding, fry it until crisp.

After the hot tortilla is removed from the heat, dip it into a sauce. Lay it on a plate or sheet of waxed paper and spoon on a filling such as shredded cheese, refried beans, green chiles, onions, or sour cream.

The next step is probably the most debated of all: Filled tortillas can be rolled, folded, or stacked.

When rolling, place the side with the loose flap down in the baking pan so it won't unroll. For stacking, simply layer the tortillas; place one on top of another about three high, spooning additional sauce over each layer. To fold, treat like a crepe, folding each long side over the filling, folding the ends if desired; place the loose ends down so they will not unravel.

To bake, follow your recipe or bake uncovered in a 350-degree oven for 20 to 30 minutes. Keep the enchiladas well moistened with sauce while heating.

AUTHOR'S NOTE: Pine nuts can be substituted for shelled pumpkin seeds. Sunflower seeds can also be used, but they are on the bitter side. The mole can be made ahead and refrigerated for up to 1 week.

~~~~~~~~~~~~

Cilantro-Seared Eggplant with Sonoran Ratatouille

Marquesa, Scottsdale Princess, Scottsdale, Arizona

CHEF REED GROBAN

SONORAN RATATOUILLE

2 tablespoons olive oil

1 tablespoon medium-diced red onion

1 ear fresh corn, kernels cut off cob

2 teaspoons finely chopped garlic

1 small red pepper, diced

1 small yellow pepper, diced

1 small fresh poblano chile, diced

1 medium zucchini, diced

1 medium yellow squash, diced

1 cup black beans, cooked (yields 3 cups of beans; or use 3 cups rinsed canned black beans)

2 plum tomatoes, diced

Salt and black pepper to taste

Heat olive oil in a large sauté pan. Add onion and corn and cook for 1 minute over moderate heat. Add garlic, peppers, and chile and sauté for 2 minutes. Add the zucchini and yellow squash and sauté for 2 minutes. Add the black beans and tomatoes. Season to taste with salt and black pepper. Keep warm while preparing eggplant.

CILANTRO-SEARED EGGPLANT

1 large eggplant, peeled and sliced into 8 equal rounds

Salt and black pepper to taste

4 tablespoons finely chopped cilantro

1 tablespoon ground cumin

1 tablespoon chili powder

¼ cup olive oil

Cilantro sprigs for garnish

4 tablespoons shredded jack cheese

Season the eggplant rounds with salt and pepper and set aside. Combine the chopped cilantro, cumin, and chili powder. Dredge eggplant in this herb and spice mixture. In a nonstick sauté pan over moderate heat, heat oil and sauté eggplant until soft.

To serve, divide the ratatouille among 4 plates and arrange 2 slices of the eggplant on each. Garnish each plate with fresh cilantro sprigs and shredded jack cheese.

SERVES 4

AUTHOR'S NOTE: Substitute ½ cup frozen corn if fresh is not available.

Polenta with Summer Vegetables and Roasted Nopales

The Range Cafe, Bernalillo, New Mexico

CHEF JAY D. WULF

POLENTA

4 to 5 cups water

1 cup uncooked polenta

Salt and pepper to taste

Red wine vinegar to taste

4 tablespoons butter

3 tablespoons grated Parmesan cheese

Bring 4 cups of the water to a slow boil in a large sauté pan and whisk in the polenta. Bring back to a simmer and reduce heat so that the mixture remains at a slow bubble. It is not necessary to stand over the pan, but stir every minute or so to avoid sticking and burning. While cooking, season lightly with salt, pepper, and a splash of vinegar.

The trickiest part to cooking polenta is knowing when it is done. With a straight 4:1 ratio of water to polenta, the polenta may be stiff when it is completely cooked. If too stiff, add a little extra water to make it a little saucier and a little less stiff. The kernels of polenta need to be "exploded." It shouldn't be "toothsome" like pasta but rather soft, like a good-quality oat when cooked.

When polenta is cooked, add the butter and the Parmesan. If kept hot, the polenta will last 2 to 3 hours, needing only a little whisk now and then and possibly a little water to adjust the consistency.

SUMMER VEGETABLES AND ROASTED NOPALES

3 to 4 cups vegetables (such as corn, green beans,
   tomatoes, eggplant, arugula, basil, baby leeks, and
   wild mushrooms)

4 medium nopales (prickly pear cactus pads)

4 tablespoons olive oil

Salt and pepper to taste

1 onion, diced into ¼-inch cubes

2 cloves garlic, minced

1 cup water

Lemon juice to taste

Chopped Italian parsley for garnish

Fresh basil for garnish

Grated Parmesan cheese for garnish

Prepare vegetables by cooking, blanching, or grilling them. For example, cut white corn off the cob or cube and grill eggplant. Set aside.

Preheat oven to 350 degrees.

Trim the edges of the nopales and dice into ¼-inch pieces. Toss nopales with enough olive oil to coat and season lightly with salt and pepper. Place on a baking tray and bake for 15 to 20 minutes. As the nopales juice seeps out, the nopales will brown a little at the edges. If they appear or feel slimy, like okra, allow them to cook a little longer. They will develop a wonderful flavor and texture.

In a large sauté pan over medium heat, combine 2 tablespoons of the olive oil, the onion, garlic, and a pinch of salt. Stew until the onion becomes translucent. Toss in the nopales and vegetables.

Add the water. The richness of the sauté will turn the water into instant vegetable stock. Bring to a slow simmer, season with salt, pepper, and lemon juice to taste.

To serve, spoon the polenta into the middle of large pasta bowls and surround with the ragout. Garnish with chopped Italian parsley or fresh basil and grated cheese.

SERVES 4 TO 6

AUTHOR'S NOTE: This is the best explanation of cooking polenta I have read. The secret is not to speed the process but to allow the kernels to expand or "explode." Once you try this, you will be hooked. It is delicious.

PRICKLY PEAR

ONE OF THE most powerful influences on Southwest food came from Native American homesites. Whether it was the Paiute, Navajo, Hopi, or Apache, Native Americans were the first to create dishes of wonder with indigenous materials, including an icon of the Southwest: the cactus. There are approximately 1,200 species of cactus. The most popular for cooking is the opuntia, or prickly pear.

Native Americans have used the prickly pear as a medicine. Peeled stems produce moisture that can be used on open wounds. Pads were once baked and used to treat ulcers and gout. The pads were cleaned of needles and baked, then tied to a mumps victim's neck to reduce swelling.

The prickly pear also shines as a valuable food source. It has saved countless lives with its bitter juice at the ready for thirsty travelers, and Native Americans ate it raw, or cooked, dried the pulp and stored it, and chewed it as a snack like gum.

Traditionally, prickly pear is harvested in late summer. When purchasing prickly pear for home use, select smaller, thicker pads as they are the most tender. Handle the pads with care—the hairlike spines can easily get trapped in flesh and cause great discomfort. To clean a prickly pear safely, hold the pad tightly with a thick towel and remove the spines with a small paring knife or vegetable peeler. Don't forget the outside edge. The resulting peel is not garbage-disposal friendly, so discard it.

One other note of caution: Prickly pear juice can stain like no other, so do not let it sit on countertops or on clothing.

Randy's Southwest Pasta

Randy's Restaurant and Bar,
Durango, Colorado

CHEF IVAN J. WALCOTT

¼ cup olive oil

½ cup sliced red, yellow, and green bell peppers

¼ cup sliced red onion

¼ cup peeled and cubed eggplant

¼ cup asparagus

⅛ cup cubed carrots

¼ cup cubed squash (mixed varieties)

2 tablespoons minced fresh garlic

2 tablespoons minced shallot

1 tablespoon chopped chipotle pepper

1 tablespoon chopped fresh cilantro

½ cup white wine

3 cups cooked penne or mostaccioli pasta

¼ cup balsamic vinegar

¼ cup Parmesan cheese

⅛ cup pumpkin seeds

Salt and white pepper to taste

Heat a large sauté pan, add olive oil, and lightly sauté bell peppers, onions, eggplant, asparagus, carrots, squash, garlic, and shallots. Vegetables should still be firm. Add chipotle pepper and cilantro. Deglaze the pan with white wine. Add fresh penne pasta or cooked mostaccioli and toss until warm. Sprinkle with balsamic vinegar and toss. Serve in a large pasta bowl topped with Parmesan cheese and pumpkin seeds. Add salt and pepper to taste.

SERVES 2

New Mexican Harvest Vegetables in Crisp Phyllo with Peach-Chile Coulis and Jalapeño-Chayote Slaw

Inn of the Anasazi, Santa Fe, New Mexico

CHEF FLYNT PAYNE

NEW MEXICAN HARVEST VEGETABLES IN CRISP PHYLLO

20 sheets (1 package) phyllo dough

About 1 pound (4 sticks) butter, melted

2 cups asadero cheese

2 winter squash, thinly sliced

2 zucchini, thinly sliced

½ sweet onion, thinly sliced

½ New Mexican or Anaheim chile, thinly sliced

1 red bell pepper, seeded and thinly sliced

¼ cup chopped cilantro

1 tablespoon chopped fresh sage (or 1 teaspoon dried)

Salt and pepper to taste

Olive oil for coating saucepan and baking sheet

Start with a single layer of phyllo dough and brush it heavily with melted butter. Stack another layer of dough on top, brushing it with butter. Repeat until there are 10 layers of dough. Do this twice to make 2 wraps. Divide cheese and, while leaving 1½ inches clear on the top edges, spread half the cheese on each wrap. Layer the

---

OPPOSITE: *New Mexican Harvest Vegetables in Crisp Phyllo with Peach-Chile Coulis and Jalapeño-Chayote Slaw*

squash, zucchini, onion, chile, and bell pepper on top. Sprinkle with cilantro, sage, salt, and pepper. Roll up tightly.

Preheat oven to 350 degrees.

Lightly coat a saucepan with olive oil and sear both rolls entirely. After searing, place rolls on a well-greased baking sheet and bake for 20 to 25 minutes.

To serve, slice the rolls into 6 or 8 slices. Lay them on a bed of Peach-Chile Coulis (recipe follows) with the Jalapeño-Chayote Slaw (recipe follows) on the side.

SERVES 6 TO 8

PEACH-CHILE COULIS

10 peaches, peeled, pitted, and sliced

2 ancho chiles, seeded and sliced

½ red onion, chopped

3 cloves garlic, minced

1 cup grapefruit juice

Juice of 2 limes

Juice of 1 lemon

1 bunch cilantro, stems removed, chopped

1 teaspoon toasted and ground coriander seeds

½ teaspoon cumin seed

1 quart apple cider

2 tablespoons ground red chili powder

Salt and pepper to taste

Combine peaches, ancho chiles, onion, and garlic. Sauté over high heat for 8 minutes. Add grapefruit juice, lime juice, lemon juice, cilantro, coriander, cumin seed, apple cider, chili powder, and salt and pepper. Reduce, uncovered, for 1 hour. Purée and strain. Adjust seasoning as desired.

JALAPEÑO-CHAYOTE SLAW

1 chayote squash, thinly sliced

1 red bell pepper, thinly sliced

4 scallions, thinly sliced

1 rib celery, thinly sliced

2 cups shredded napa cabbage

¼ cup honey

½ cup white vinegar

3 jalapeños, minced

2 tablespoons cilantro leaves

¼ ounce "gold" tequila

Salt and pepper to taste

Combine chayote squash, bell pepper, scallions, celery, and cabbage. In a separate bowl, whisk together honey, vinegar, jalapeños, cilantro, tequila, and salt and pepper. Pour over the vegetables and toss to combine.

AUTHOR'S NOTE: Substitute Anaheim for New Mexican chiles if they are not available in your area. Both the coulis and slaw may be made a day ahead and refrigerated until needed. Be sure to save the material left in the coulis strainer. It is superb as an appetizer or mixed on a salad. If searing the phyllo rolls is impractical, simply omit this step and bake. It will not be as crispy but it will work.

Potato Terrine with Roasted Poblano Chile Sabayon

Nellies, Hotel Loretto, Santa Fe, New Mexico

CULINARY STAFF

POTATO TERRINE

- 2 tablespoons olive oil
- 1 tablespoon chopped garlic
- 3 shallots, minced
- 2 pounds assorted wild mushrooms, cleaned and chopped
- 1 tablespoon fresh thyme (or 1 teaspoon dried)
- 1 bunch Italian parsley
- ½ cup good brandy
- 2 tablespoons sherry wine vinegar
- 4 russet potatoes, sliced into flat, ⅛-inch-thick rectangles
- 1 cup heavy cream

Butter, at room temperature, for coating terrine

Salt and pepper to taste

Heat olive oil in a heavy-bottomed saucepan over high heat until smoking. Lower heat, add the garlic and the shallots, and sauté until soft. Add the mushrooms, thyme, and parsley, and sauté until the mushrooms release their juices. Deglaze with brandy and vinegar. Remove from heat and place mushroom mixture in the top of a double boiler. Cook slowly, uncovered, for at least an hour, until all of the mushroom liquid is evaporated. Remove from heat and cool.

Toss potatoes with the cream and divide into four portions. Brush a terrine with butter. Shake excess cream off the potatoes and layer one portion in the bottom of the pan, making sure there are no spaces. Season with salt and pepper.

Divide the mushroom mixture into thirds. Layer one third onto the first layer of potatoes. Place another layer of potatoes on top of the mushrooms, again with no spaces. Continue layering, ending with potatoes.

Preheat oven to 350 degrees.

Cover the terrine with buttered aluminum foil. Weight with an empty bread pan. Bake for one hour. Remove from heat and cool completely, so it will slice easily. Slice into 6 square portions.

To serve, reheat by sautéeing in clarified butter, turning once, until golden. Finish in a preheated oven at 350 degrees for 5 minutes. Serve hot. Top with Roasted Poblano Chile Sabayon (recipe follows).

SERVES 6

ROASTED POBLANO CHILE SABAYON

3 poblano peppers, roasted, peeled, and seeded
1 cup olive oil
2 tablespoons lemon juice
3 tablespoons white wine
3 egg yolks
Salt and white pepper to taste

In a blender or food processor, purée the poblano peppers with the olive oil. Set this mixture aside.

In a small, heavy-bottomed saucepan, combine lemon juice and 2 tablespoons of the white wine. Cook over high heat, reducing liquid to about 1 tablespoon. Remove from heat and add remaining 1 tablespoon of white wine. Beat egg yolks lightly and whisk into the lemon-wine mixture. Over low heat, whisk in the poblano purée a tablespoon at a time, incorporating each addition before adding more. Continue to cook and whisk the sauce until it is thick. Add salt and pepper to taste.

AUTHOR'S NOTE: A terrine is an earthenware dish soaked in water before use. However, today it also means a dish holding various stew-like dishes. You may use a rectangular loaf pan.

To clarify butter, melt in a saucepan and skim foam off of top. Pour into ovenproof glass dish and discard remaining fat in saucepan.

See "deglazing" in the glossary for information on this process.

ONIONS

THE ONION'S VALUE as a health food goes back at least to the third or fourth century B.C. Hippocrates declared onions good for the sight but, strangely, not the body. The Middle Ages brought a reversal of sorts, with physicians using onions to cure dog bites and insect stings. Later, onions were declared a wonderful cure for complexion difficulties.

Onions are bulbs and are related to the sweetly fragrant tulip and lily-of-the-valley. They are also closely aligned with garlic and chives. Most varieties are available year-round, but the popular Bermuda and Spanish onions are usually only on grocery shelves from late spring through early fall.

Wild onions have been enormously popular with virtually all residents of the Southwest. Since they are so easy to find and gather, onions have been used in foods as well as medicines. Early explorers of the Southwest wrote of how easy it was to locate some tribal encampments due to the heavy aroma of cooking onions. Native Americans roasted the bulbs in cooking pits, dried them, and then tied them into bundles for later use.

Choose only firm onions: Soft means spoiled. If they are sprouting, they will have little flavor and a horrid texture.

Keep onions away from the refrigerator. They store best in hanging baskets or where air can circulate. Keep them in the dark, too. Direct light causes onions to produce chlorophyll, and this makes them bitter.

Grilled Polenta and
Southwestern Ratatouille

Cottage Place Restaurant,
Flagstaff, Arizona

CHEF FRANK BRANHAM

GRILLED POLENTA

- 1 cup cornmeal
- 4 cups water
- 1 tablespoon salt
- 1 teaspoon cumin
- ⅛ teaspoon cayenne
- 1 cup shredded Monterey jack cheese
- 2 teaspoons fresh cilantro
- Vegetable oil spray, as needed

Soak cornmeal with 1 cup of the water. Bring the remaining 3 cups of water to a boil in a medium saucepan. Add salt, cumin, and cayenne to boiling water. Add the blended cornmeal to boiling water. Stir polenta vigorously as it comes to a boil. Turn down heat and cover. Cook polenta for at least 20 minutes. While it's cooking, remove cover periodically and stir. After 20 minutes, add cheese and cilantro and stir until polenta is smooth and creamy.

Spray a 9-inch pie pan with vegetable oil. Pour polenta into the pan and smooth the top with a spatula. Chill for 1 hour. Cut chilled polenta into 8 wedges.

Preheat a barbecue grill. Spray polenta wedges with vegetable spray and grill them until they are well marked and hot. Spoon Southwestern Ratatouille (recipe follows) into the centers of four plates and set grilled polenta wedges on ratatouille.

SERVES 4

SOUTHWESTERN RATATOUILLE

    2 teaspoons olive oil
    ¼ cup diced onion
    1 teaspoon minced garlic
    1 cup diced zucchini
    1 cup diced tomato
    ½ cup corn kernels
    2 tablespoons ancho chile (dried poblano) purée (recipe
      follows)
    1 teaspoon salt
    ½ teaspoon cumin
    2 teaspoons fresh cilantro

In a sauté pan, heat olive oil and sauté onion and garlic until onions are translucent. Add zucchini and sauté several minutes. Add diced tomato, corn, and chile purée. Sauté gently, then season with salt, cumin, and cilantro. Keep warm.

ANCHO CHILE PURÉE

    1 (2-ounce) package ancho chiles
    1 cup water

Remove seeds, stems, and inner membrane of chiles.
Bring water to a boil in a small saucepan. Add chiles. Simmer 5 minutes. Turn heat off and let chiles steam, covered, 30 minutes. Purée chiles in water. Strain.

AUTHOR'S NOTE: This is a spicy dish. To cut down on the heat, consider eliminating the cayenne from the polenta or substituting white pepper and using less ancho chile purée in the ratatouille.

Chipotle Crema Morel Stew in Acorn Squash

Cafe Pasqual's, Santa Fe, New Mexico

CHEF KATHARINE KAGEL

SQUASH

> 8 acorn squash

Sever squash tops, leaving stems attached, removing seeds and strings and reserving them for stock.

VEGETABLE STOCK

> ¾ pound small red potatoes
> ¼ cup olive oil
> 3 cloves garlic, coarsely chopped
> Celery leaves from one bunch of celery, roughly chopped
> 4 small yellow onions, quartered
> Seeds and strings from acorn squash
> 2½ quarts water

Peel potatoes. Set aside the peels for this stock and the potatoes for the stew (recipe follows).

In a stock pot over medium heat, heat the olive oil and add the garlic, celery leaves, potato peels, onions, and squash seeds and string. Sauté until lightly browned. Add water and bring to a rolling boil. Skim off any foam that forms and discard. Simmer stock, uncovered, for one hour. Strain stock through a strainer and set aside for the stew (recipe follows).

CHIPOTLE CREMA MOREL STEW

> 2 tablespoons fresh chipotle *en adobado* (canned in vinegar)
> 3 cups heavy cream
> 2 tablespoons olive oil

1 cup cubed carrots (½ inch)

1 cup cubed rutabagas (½ inch)

½ cup sliced celery stalks

1½ cups cubed zucchini or summer squash (½ inch)

Reserved peeled potatoes, cut into ½-inch cubes

2 portabello mushrooms, stems and gills removed, thinly sliced

1 cup fresh morels (or dried morels hydrated in hot water for 20 minutes), quartered

1 clove garlic, finely minced

2 teaspoons peeled and grated ginger

Vegetable stock

Purée chipotle *en adobado* in a blender or food processor and strain through a mesh sieve to remove seeds. Set aside. Simmer cream until reduced by half. Set aside.

Preheat oven to 350 degrees.

In a large saucepan, sauté remaining ingredients except the stock for 10 minutes. Add the stock and simmer for 10 minutes or until the squash is fork tender. Add reduced cream to chipotle purée and stir until combined. Pour mixture over sautéed vegetables and gently mix in until well incorporated.

Place prepared acorn squash on a baking sheet. Fill each with water and cover with its top. Bake for 1 hour or until fork tender.

Fill the baked acorn squashes with the stew. Serve with the tops on and with garlic toast or other toasted bread.

SERVES 8

AUTHOR'S NOTE: A fun presentation to delight your guests: To maximize the use of the stew, carve out some of the acorn squash "meat" after cooking and add it to the purée. For a richer appearance, rub the outside of the squash with olive oil before baking.

OPPOSITE: *Three-Pepper Polenta Bread (recipe page 156) and Chipotle Crema Morel Stew in Acorn Squash (recipe page 119)*

Red Chile and Jalapeño Fettucine with Cilantro Cream and Toasted Walnuts

Garland's Oak Creek Lodge, Sedona, Arizona

CHEF AMANDA STINE

RED CHILE FETTUCINE

- 2 cups unbleached flour, plus flour for rolling dough
- 4 tablespoons ground red chile
- 2 teaspoons ground cumin
- 2 teaspoons salt
- 4 large eggs

Place 2 cups flour, ground red chile, cumin, and salt in a food processor and pulse a few times to mix. Break the eggs into the processor and blend continuously until mixture forms a ball or a mass on the sides of the processor bowl. Turn out the dough onto a lightly floured surface and knead it until smooth and somewhat elastic. Knead in extra flour as necessary—the dough should not be too damp or too dry. Wrap dough in plastic and set it aside to rest for 10 minutes.

JALAPEÑO FETTUCINE

- 2 cups unbleached flour, plus flour for rolling dough
- 2 tablespoons finely minced jalapeños
- 2 teaspoons salt
- 3 to 4 eggs

lace flour, chiles, and salt in a food processor and pulse a few times to mix. Add 3 eggs, process, then add part or all of the fourth egg. Process until the dough mass comes together, then turn out onto a lightly floured surface. To adjust consistency, knead in more flour by hand. This dough is typically wetter than the red chile fettucine dough. When smooth, wrap the dough in plastic and set it aside to rest.

Process both doughs on a pasta machine, taking each portion through 1 to 6 settings. The smallest setting is too thin for fettuccine. Hang the pasta to dry while preparing the cream sauce.

CILANTRO CREAM

¼ cup virgin olive oil

6 cloves garlic, finely minced

1 cup vegetable stock

1 cup heavy cream

Kosher salt to taste

⅓ cup chopped cilantro

Freshly ground black pepper

½ to 1 cup grated Parmesan

¾ cup toasted, chopped walnuts or pecans

ombine oil, garlic, and stock in a saucepan. Bring to a boil and reduce for about 2 minutes. Add cream and simmer for 3 to 4 minutes until sauce thickens somewhat. Add salt. Keep warm while pasta cooks, adding cilantro just before pouring sauce over freshly cooked pasta. Season with several grinds of pepper, and toss with Parmesan and walnuts. Serve immediately on warmed plates or in bowls. Pass extra grated Parmesan.

SERVES 4

AUTHOR'S NOTE: If you don't have the time or inclination to make the pasta from scratch, purchase fresh, flavored pasta. Unlike dried pasta, fresh pasta cooks in boiling water in only a few minutes, so check for doneness frequently.

VEGETABLE STOCKS

MANY RECIPES IN this book call for vegetable stocks. While fresh stocks are time consuming to create, anyone who can start a flame under a pot can make a stock. Some cooks may opt to purchase a canned stock, which will suffice. However, no canned broth or stock can compare with the fresh flavor of real stock. Many foods prepared at home do not have the rich flavor of those sampled at good restaurants because of, at least in part, the hearty fresh stocks commercial chefs create for their dishes.

Stocks originated in the kitchens of the poor since almost any piece of vegetable, or meat, could go into a stock—a very economical approach to preparing a tasty dish. Today stocks are still often made with both vegetables and meat. The vegetables impart a crisp, fresh flavor, and the meat and bones provide a hearty flavor and thickening agent. But meats and poultry are not necessary for a flavorful or complete stock. An outstanding stock can be made with only vegetables.

While good recipes abound on how to make a stock from scratch, many restaurants just keep a pot of simmering water next to the preparation area, and all the ends, stalks, and vegetable pieces left over from cutting up ingredients are thrown into that pot, including seeds and stems.

Cooking a stock is a very simple procedure. Start with a large, heavy-bottomed pot, such as a Dutch oven. Fill the pot about halfway with water and bring it to a slow simmer. Add fresh vegetable pieces and/or vegetable scraps. Simmer, uncovered, for a clear, brothlike stock, but be careful not to boil it down too quickly. To slow down evaporation, partially cover the stock, allowing some but not all of the steam to escape.

When rich in flavor, strain well and cool quickly to avoid spoiling. (Placing the stock in smaller dishes and setting them in ice is one method for rapid cooling.) Cooled and refrigerated immediately, the stock should last about five days, but be sure to boil it again before use. Frozen, stocks can last up to six months, and most stocks do freeze well.

If you make an extra-large batch, after straining divide and freeze the stock in 6-ounce portions. Even larger blocks may be handy. Some cooks freeze the stock in an ice tray and place the frozen cubes in freezer bags, taking out only what they need when they need it.

Most good cookbooks contain good stock recipes. Try one and see what a difference it makes in your cooking.

Southwestern Vegetable Stew with Black Olive Sauce

Christopher's and Christopher's Bistro, Phoenix, Arizona

CHEF CHRISTOPHER J. GROSS

8 plum tomatoes, halved

Salt and pepper to taste

2 zucchini, sliced into ½-inch pieces

2 yellow squash, sliced into ½-inch pieces

3 medium artichokes, steamed

3 tablespoons olive oil

2 cloves garlic, minced

2 red bell peppers, roasted, seeded, and diced into
    ½-inch pieces

16 small asparagus tips

1 quart vegetable stock (about 2½ 13¾-ounce cans)

1 tablespoon chopped cilantro

1 tablespoon chopped fresh oregano (or 1 teaspoon dried)

1 tablespoon chopped fresh basil (or 1 teaspoon dried),
    plus four leaves

1 tablespoon chopped fresh thyme (or 1 teaspoon dried)

Salt and pepper to taste

2 cups whole pitted black olives

Preheat oven to 225 degrees.

Place tomatoes cut side down on a cookie sheet. Season with salt and pepper to taste. Dry in oven for 6 to 7 hours or overnight. Reheat in a pan over the grill or in the oven.

Grill the zucchini and yellow squash slices, then dice.

Clean the artichokes, leaving the stems and the hearts and discarding the outer leaves. Cut each cleaned artichoke into eighths.

In a medium saucepan, using 2 tablespoons of the olive oil, sauté the artichokes with the minced garlic. Add the zucchini and yellow squash and toss to coat. Add the red bell peppers, asparagus tips, and dried tomatoes and barely cover with vegetable stock. Let simmer over medium heat for 4 to 5 minutes and strain, reserving the stock. Place the vegetables back in the pot and add cilantro, oregano, basil, thyme, and salt and pepper. Stir until blended, then set aside, keeping warm.

Take the stock used to cook the vegetables and place in a pot with the remainder of the vegetable stock. Add the black olives. Simmer until the mixture has been reduced by one-half. Blend thoroughly and strain.

Spoon the warm vegetables into the centers of four bowls (leave space between the vegetables and the edges of the bowls). Spoon olive sauce around the vegetables. Fry basil leaves in the remaining tablespoon of olive oil, then place one on top of each mound of vegetables as a garnish.

SERVES 4

AUTHOR'S NOTE: While this may sound time-consuming, most of the waiting time is drying the tomatoes. If time is of the essence, purchase dried tomatoes and reconstitute them. See "Roasting Chile Peppers," page 10, to learn more about preparing peppers.

SQUASH

NATIVE TO THE western hemisphere but not to the Southwest, squash is still astoundingly popular as a basic food. It is likely squash migrated from South America, eventually to grow wild throughout the United States. It became not only a handy ingredient in cuisine but also a valuable trading commodity.

Squash is second only to corn as an important ingredient in traditional Native American and early Mexican diets. Early Southwestern residents normally consumed the entire squash, including skins, meat, and seeds. Squash was cooked whole in the ashes of fire pits, boiled until tender, or dried in the sun. Then and now, hardier types of squash are dried and made into rattles and other ritualistic instruments.

All squashes are gourds and are divided into two main types: winter and summer. The differences are more than just growing season. Summer squashes are typically harvested immature so the seeds and rinds are tender; winter squashes are harvested mature, so seeds are generally tough and rinds even tougher. Summer squashes include crookneck, pattypan, and zucchini. Winter squash varieties include butternut, acorn, and pumpkin. Today, many squashes are crossbred just for their interesting colors and used to adorn shelves and kitchen counters.

Winter squash should feel hard and be blemish free and rich in color. Summer squash should have fresh, tender rinds and be free of blemishes. Both will feel heavy for their size. Summer squash will not keep as long—usually no more than two weeks—as the winter variety. Some winter squash will last up to four weeks if kept in a cool, dry area.

Eggplant Cannelloni with Roasted Tomato Coulis and Tatsoi Salad

Michael's at the Citadel, Scottsdale, Arizona

CHEF MICHAEL J. DEMARIA

EGGPLANT CANNELLONI

2 medium eggplants

Salt for leaching eggplants

3 tablespoons olive oil

2 bulbs garlic, peeled and chopped

3 portabello mushrooms

Ice water for blanched asparagus

30 asparagus spears

6 ounces goat cheese

1 teaspoon chopped fresh rosemary (or ¼ teaspoon dried)

2 teaspoons chopped fresh basil (or ½ teaspoon dried)

2 teaspoons chopped fresh parsley (or ½ teaspoon dried)

Black pepper to taste

Slice the ends off the eggplants, peel, and cut widthwise into ¼-inch slices. Lay eggplant slices on a drip rack and sprinkle some salt on both sides. Let stand at room temperature for 3 to 4 hours, or until the eggplant appears translucent. Rinse off the salt and pat dry.

Preheat a grill.

Place eggplant slices on the hot grill and make "X" grill marks on one side. Remove slices from the grill and set aside to cool.

Mix the olive oil with half the garlic and set aside.

Cut the stems off the mushrooms. Using a spoon, scrape the black gills off the underside of each mushroom and brush caps with the olive oil mixture. Grill mushrooms over medium flame until they are tender and juicy, about 7 to 10 minutes. Remove them from the grill and allow to cool. Slice them into 4-inch-long pieces and set aside.

Boil water for blanching asparagus. Prepare ice water to stop the blanching.

Starting at the tips, cut asparagus into 4-inch lengths. Blanch asparagus spears in boiling water for 1 minute, then shock in ice water until cool. Remove and set aside. (Note: Any remaining asparagus spears can be used for salads or soups or sautéed for a sidedish.)

In a small bowl, whip goat cheese. (A hand mixer works fine.) Add remaining garlic, rosemary, basil, parsley, and black pepper. Place mixture in a pastry bag for piping onto the cannelloni.

Preheat oven to 350 degrees.

Arrange the eggplant slices in rows for assembly. On each slice, place 4 pieces of asparagus and 2 portabello slices. Then pipe a 2-inch tube of the goat cheese mixture down the center. Place 2 more portabello slices on top of the cheese. Roll up the cannelloni and place seam side down in a baking dish. Bake, covered, for 30 minutes, or steam.

To serve, spoon 2 ounces of warm tomato coulis (recipe follows) on the center of each plate. Place one cannelloni on each plate in the twelve o'clock position. Place a second cannelloni at the ten o'clock position, so that they are stacked diagonally. Then pile tatsoi salad (recipe follows) over the top, allowing it to fall over and down the cannelloni.

SERVES 4

ROASTED TOMATO COULIS

   4 large tomatoes (beefsteak size)
   1 cup olive oil
   Salt and pepper to taste

Grill tomatoes with core intact until they are cooked all around. Then put the tomatoes into a pan and allow them to cool, reserving all the juices. When they are cool, place the tomatoes in a food processor and pulse until they begin to form a purée. Add olive oil slowly through the top until the purée starts to thicken. Stop processing and test the purée by dipping a spoon into it. If the sauce coats the spoon, it is done. Add salt and pepper to taste. Set aside until dish is ready to assemble.

TATSOI SALAD

4 ounces tatsoi (baby bok choy), torn apart
1 piece of red onion, peeled
2 tablespoons balsamic vinegar
¼ cup olive oil
Kosher salt to taste
Black pepper to taste

Clean, wash, and dry the tatsoi. Place it in a bowl with red onion. Toss with balsamic vinegar and olive oil. Add salt and black pepper.

AUTHOR'S NOTE: This dish is much easier than it sounds. You can use a hot skillet to brown eggplant. If unable to find a pastry bag to "pipe" whipped goat cheese, simply spoon it on evenly.

Grilled Portabello Mushrooms with Southwestern Black Beans, Corn Relish, and Goat Cheese

Eddie's Grill, Phoenix, Arizona

CHEF EDDIE MATNEY

GRILLED PORTABELLO MUSHROOMS

½ cup Eddie's Herbed Olive Oil (recipe follows)

2 tablespoons balsamic vinegar

2 portabello mushrooms, stems removed

8 ounces goat cheese

Southwestern Black Beans (recipe follows)

Corn Relish (recipe follows)

4 sprigs cilantro

Combine herbed olive oil and vinegar; marinate mushrooms for 3 hours.

Preheat a grill. Grill mushrooms until soft; slice into ½-inch-thick strips.

Shape cheese into four 2-ounce balls; heat gently in a nonstick pan over low heat. To serve, ladle a ½ cup of warm black beans and a ¼ cup of warm corn relish onto each of 4 large plates. Skewer mushroom strips and lay skewers in a circular manner around each plate. Place 1 cheese ball in the center; garnish with cilantro sprig.

SERVES 4

OPPOSITE: *Grilled Portabello Mushrooms with Southwestern Black Beans, Corn Relish, and Goat Cheese*

EDDIE'S HERBED OLIVE OIL

2 cups extra virgin olive oil

8 large cloves garlic

24 fresh basil leaves

6 sprigs fresh sage

4 sprigs fresh oregano

6 sprigs fresh parsley

6 sprigs fresh thyme

½ cup roasted pine nuts

¼ cup shredded Parmesan cheese

Juice from 1 large lemon

2 tablespoons salt

1 tablespoon pepper

Pinch cayenne pepper

Combine half of the ingredients in a blender; chop. Repeat with remaining ingredients; blend two halves together. Mixture should be chunky and green. Oil mixture will keep at room temperature for 1 day; if refrigerated, 2 weeks.

YIELDS 3 CUPS

SOUTHWESTERN BLACK BEANS

¼ cup butter

1 large onion, chopped

¼ cup chopped shallot

¼ cup chopped garlic

2 pounds black beans, soaked overnight

1 gallon vegetable stock (about 9½ 13¾-ounce cans)

1 tablespoon ground black pepper

1 teaspoon celery salt

2 cups white vinegar

I In a large stock pot over medium heat, sauté onion, shallots, and garlic in butter until tender. Add beans and coat with butter. Add stock, pepper, and celery salt. Cook, uncovered, for 4 hours or until beans are tender and liquid is reduced. Fold in vinegar; simmer 10 minutes.

SERVES 8 TO 10

CORN RELISH

1 cup frozen corn kernels
2 tablespoons olive oil
¼ cup diced roasted green chiles
¼ cup diced red bell pepper
Salt and pepper to taste.

I n a skillet over medium heat, caramelize corn in oil until golden brown. Drain corn. Add remaining ingredients.

YIELDS 1 CUP

AUTHOR'S NOTE: For variety, the Southwest Black Beans recipe can be doubled. Use chiles in one half and green bell pepper in the other half for non-chile lovers. The black beans may take longer to cook if they are older beans. Save any remaining beans for another meal or recipe.

MUSHROOMS

The MOST POPULAR mushroom in use today is the button mushroom, or *champignon de Paris*. Although not native to the Southwest, two of the most popular additions to Southwestern entrees are the portabello and shiitake.

Historically, few Native Americans used mushrooms. Unable to distinguish the toxic from the tasty, most left well enough alone. However, in the Southwest, where there were fewer wild varieties to choose among, mushrooms were more popular. Modern chefs have seen fit to expand their use because the added flavor cannot be duplicated by anything else.

Members of the fungus family, mushrooms are an astoundingly simple life form, reproducing by spores spread in the wind. They are renowned for subsisting on decaying matter and provide an important recycling service in forests.

When selecting fresh mushrooms, keep in mind they are highly perishable. Pick ones with smooth, unblemished caps. Button mushroom caps should be firm to a light squeeze.

Refrigerate mushrooms unwashed, wrapped tightly in paper towels; they should last about two days. Never store in plastic bags because trapped moisture will cause rapid deterioration. If your schedule dictates longer storage before use, cook the mushrooms first, then freeze in an airtight container; they should be good for a month or two.

Mushrooms will absorb moisture and take in the flavors of almost any dish. This is one of the reasons they should not be washed in water before inclusion in a recipe: They will quickly fill with water instead of the desirable seasoning.

Since today's mushrooms are grown in sterilized soil, just brush off any remaining dirt.

Vegetarian Anasazi Beans

Manzanita Restaurant,
Cornville, Arizona

CHEF ALBERT KRAMER

2 cups dried Anasazi beans

5 cups vegetable broth or water

¼ teaspoon salt

Black pepper to taste

¼ teaspoon ground cumin

¼ teaspoon nutmeg

4 cloves garlic, pressed

1 bay leaf

¼ cup olive oil

½ cup diced celery

½ cup diced onion

½ cup seeded and diced green bell pepper

½ cup seeded and diced red bell pepper

1 tablespoon tomato paste

Soak Anasazi beans in warm water in a large pot for one hour prior to cooking. Cook beans in vegetable broth or water with the salt, pepper, cumin, nutmeg, 2 cloves garlic, and bay leaf for 30 minutes. Meanwhile, sauté the remaining garlic, celery, onion, and peppers in olive oil until translucent but still crisp. Add vegetables to the semicooked beans along with tomato paste. Cook for another 30 minutes until tender.

Serve in a large soup bowl with a salad on the side. Can be topped with Parmesan if desired.

SERVES 4 TO 6

AUTHOR'S NOTE: Thoroughly cooking beans is a simple process, but the timing is highly variable because the moisture content in dried beans varies widely. If your beans are old, the cooking may take longer, so cook as long as necessary until tender.

This also makes an excellent side dish to many other recipes.

Lentil Cakes

Rancho Pinot Grill, Scottsdale, Arizona

CHEF CHRYSA KAUFMAN

LENTILS

6 cups water

½ pound green or brown lentils

2 tablespoons finely diced onion

1 clove garlic, minced

½ teaspoon salt

1 bay leaf

Place water, lentils, onion, garlic, salt, and bay leaf in a large pot over high heat. Bring to a boil, reduce heat, and simmer 40 minutes until the lentils are cooked through and tender, but still holding their shape. Don't drain the little liquid that remains. Let lentils cool to room temperature. Remove the bay leaf.

CAKES

1 small baking potato

2 tablespoons olive oil

2 carrots, grated

½ onion, diced small

2 cloves garlic, minced

1 teaspoon ground cumin

½ teaspoon ground coriander

½ teaspoon oregano

1 teaspoon chili powder (more or less, according to desired heat)

1 teaspoon salt

2 tablespoons chopped fresh cilantro

2 tablespoons fresh lime juice

1 cup plus 2 to 4 tablespoons bread crumbs

2 tablespoons canola oil

1 cup Yogurt Sauce (recipe follows)

Preheat oven to 350 degrees while lentils are cooking.

Bake potato for 45 to 60 minutes (or 7 to 10 minutes in microwave) until tender. Let cool. Remove and discard skin.

Place the olive oil in a skillet over medium heat. Add carrots, onion, and garlic. Cook about 5 minutes until softened. Add cumin, coriander, oregano, chili powder, and salt. Heat for a moment until fragrant.

Stir the lentils and potato into the pan and mash them with a fork to thoroughly incorporate the potato, leaving some of the lentils intact. Stir in cilantro and lime juice. Add just enough bread crumbs to hold the mixture together, about 2 to 4 tablespoons.

Remove the mixture from the skillet and set it on a cookie sheet to cool.

Form cakes ½-inch thick and 2 inches in diameter. Place 1 cup bread crumbs in a dish. Press the patties into the bread crumbs until coated.

Heat the oil in a skillet over medium-high heat. Set the patties in the skillet. Cook 2 to 3 minutes on each side until browned and crispy.

Serve topped with Yogurt Sauce (recipe follows), and salad greens on the side.

SERVES 6 TO 8

YOGURT SAUCE

1 cup plain yogurt

1 tablespoon lime juice

½ cucumber, seeded and diced

2 green onions, sliced

1 teaspoon chopped fresh mint

1 teaspoon chopped fresh cilantro

½ teaspoon coarsely ground black pepper

½ teaspoon salt

Combine all ingredients.

YIELDS I CUP

HOMINY

MANY WITH LITTLE experience in Southwestern lore believe hominy to be a dish created in the deep South as a side to a host of entrées. Hominy was actually created by Native Americans. It is hulled, dried corn from which the germ has been removed. Usually sold in bulk, it is also available canned. Ground, it is well-known in the south as "grits." In Mexican markets, hominy may be called *pozole*.

As a hard, dried corn, hominy must first be softened by cooking in water or milk. Then the corn may be fried, baked, or served as a sauce.

The biggest advantage of dried hominy is its storage life. Properly dried, it will last almost indefinitely. This long shelf life carried many tribes and villages through difficult winters.

Preparation of hominy generally includes soaking it overnight in water, much like beans. After soaking, lightly salt the water and cook over low heat for 4 to 5 hours, stirring often, until the hulls are loose. Keep the hominy covered with water to prevent scorching. When ready, use it in the recipe of your choice.

Breads

Breads of the Southwest were usually either sourdough or quick breads. Early residents of the Southwest needed an easily accessible leavening agent. No store held anything resembling the packaged yeast we purchase today.

The most popular starter, sourdough, was a living, active yeast. It was protected like a precious jewel: fed, nurtured and kept warm. European in creation, the sponge provided a delectable starter for many varieties of Southwestern breads. Ranchers, cattlemen and pioneers attempted to carry the starter on every extended trip from home.

On the other hand, quick breads were artificially leavened with a chemical like baking soda or baking powder. Within a few years of the chemical leavening's discovery, it quickly surpassed sourdoughs as the agent of choice. Breads were easily made anywhere there was a fire. They still exist today as muffins and biscuits.

Finally, some recipes of the early Southwest contained no leavening agent at all, or a very weak one. Most Native American breads used little or no agents to soften textures until Europeans introduced wheat to this area.

Here are a few representations for breads. These recipes combine the talents of leading contemporary bakers of the Southwest, all with a Southwestern flavor complementing many dishes in this book. Most are very simple to assemble. They also vary in size, meaning some recipes make five loaves, some only two. I have not modified these recipes because many of the ingredients are so dependent on each other that changing them in any way may affect the original intent of their creators.

OPPOSITE: *Clockwise from top: Three-Pepper Polenta Bread (recipe page 156), Southwest Bread (recipe page 151), Chocolate-Raspberry Muffins (page 145), Atalaya's Green Chile-Apple-Cheddar Sourdough (page 148), and Pepper-Corn Muffins (page 144).*

Pepper-Corn Muffins

Golden Swan, Hyatt Regency, Scottsdale, Arizona

CHEF ANTON BRUNBAUER

2 onions, finely chopped
1 green bell pepper, finely chopped
½ red bell pepper, finely chopped
1 green chile, finely chopped
Butter for sautéing
¼ pound (1 stick) butter
½ cup sugar
2 whole eggs
2 cups bread flour
6 teaspoons baking powder, sifted
3 teaspoons baking soda, sifted
2 teaspoons salt
2 cups cornmeal
1 cup milk
10 ounces grated cheese of your choice
4 ounces grated Parmesan cheese

In a saucepan, sauté chopped onions, red and green peppers, and green chile in butter until tender, then drain and cool. Preheat oven to 350 degrees.

Cream the stick of butter and sugar together. Add eggs and continue to mix. Add sifted bread flour, baking powder, baking soda, and salt. Add cornmeal and milk, and continue to mix. Add sautéed vegetables and grated cheeses, incorporating them well. Bake for 25 minutes or until lightly browned.

YIELDS 36 MUFFINS

AUTHOR'S NOTE: Bread flour is a high-gluten flour and is available in most grocery stores. You can easily substitute all-purpose flour if desired.

The chef told me he was tired of trying corn muffins so dry "that dust would come out of my ears." So he developed this moist muffin that is exceptionally popular at the restaurant. Also, finely chopped vegetables will ensure that these muffins turn out exceptionally well.

~~~~~~~~~~

Chocolate–Raspberry Muffins

Double Rainbow Bakery Cafe, Albuquerque, New Mexico

BAKER JEAN BERNSTEIN

½ pound (2 sticks) butter
2 cups granulated sugar, plus some to sprinkle on top of muffins
4 large eggs
1 cup buttermilk
½ cup orange juice
4 cups all-purpose flour
2 teaspoons baking powder
1 teaspoon baking soda
1 teaspoon salt
1 (12-ounce) package semisweet chocolate chips
½ (12-ounce) package frozen raspberries or ¾ cup fresh raspberries

Cream together butter and sugar. Add eggs and beat until smooth. Stir in buttermilk and orange juice. In a separate bowl, combine flour, baking powder, baking soda, and salt. Beat dry mixture into the liquid mixture. Carefully fold in chocolate chips and raspberries until evenly distributed.

Preheat oven to 325 degrees.

Spoon batter into well-greased, large muffin tin, filling wells about three-quarters full. Sprinkle granulated sugar on top. Bake for about 25 minutes. Rotate pans and bake 15 minutes more. Muffins are done when a toothpick or skewer inserted in the center of a muffin comes out clean.

YIELDS 12 LARGE MUFFINS

AUTHOR'S NOTE: The baker uses fresh New Mexico raspberries in season. You can use also use 6 ounces frozen raspberries. Fold partially thawed raspberries in very carefully, just before adding the batter to the muffin tins. Too much stirring will turn the entire batter a light "raspberry" color. If you use a standard muffin tin instead of an extra-large one, this recipe will yield at least 18 muffins.

~~~~~~~~~~~~~~~~

Jalapeño Cheese Bread

The Village Baker, Flagstaff, Arizona

BAKER RICK HEENAN

6 cups unbleached wheat flour

1 cup stone-ground whole wheat flour

3 cups water

½ cup sugar

½ ounce yeast

1 teaspoon salt

Diced jalapeño peppers to taste (about ¼ cup)

1 large red bell pepper, diced

1 large green bell pepper, diced

½ pound Monterey jack cheese, diced into ½-inch cubes

½ pound Cheddar cheese, diced into ½-inch cubes

C ombine and mix flours, water, and sugar. If mixing by hand, add the flours slowly and mix for 10 minutes. If using an electric mixer, mix ingredients for 5 minutes.

Knead in yeast, then salt. Knead in jalapeños, bell peppers, and cheese.

Let the dough rise in a deep, greased, covered container for 1 to 2 hours, until volume is doubled. Deflate dough by punching it down.

Wait 10 to 20 minutes and cut to desired weight (typically 1 to 2 pounds). Roll into rounds, cover with loose plastic wrap, and allow a second rise (generally half the time of the first rise).

Preheat oven to 425 degrees.

Form into loaves by patting each round into a rough rectangle and tightly rolling it toward you to produce a smooth top. Pinch seams together to close. Place into well-greased bread pans, seam side down. The dough should fill one-half to two-thirds of each pan. Cover loaves with loose plastic wrap and let them rise to just over the pan lips.

Bake about 1 hour until golden brown. Check loaves by tapping bottoms of bread pans—a hollow sound indicates the breads are ready.

YIELDS 10-POUND BATCH

Atalaya's Green Chile—Apple—Cheddar Sourdough

Atalaya Restaurant and Bakery, Santa Fe, New Mexico

CHEF XUBI WILSON

1½ cups white sourdough starter (the consistency of a
   thick pancake batter)

2 cups cold water

5 cups bread flour (can use all-purpose flour, but more
   gluten is better)

3 cups whole wheat flour, plus extra for working with dough

1 tablespoon salt

⅛ cup honey

⅛ cup corn oil

⅛ cup diced green chiles (such as New Mexico green chiles)

¾ cup seeded and diced apples (such as Granny Smith)

¾ cup diced cheese (such as white Cheddar)

Vegetable oil for oiling bowl

Cornmeal for sprinkling on baking trays

In an electric mixer with dough hook attachment, combine starter and water, then add flours. Mix on medium for 5 minutes. Add salt and mix on medium for 2 minutes. Add honey, corn oil, and green chiles and mix on slow for 3 minutes. Add more flour if necessary to keep dough away from bowl sides. Add apples and cheese and mix on slow for 2 minutes or until cheese and apples are fully incorporated.

The dough may be slightly wet. Knead it into a ball, adding a small amount of flour as necessary to keep it from sticking. Place it in a lightly oiled bowl twice its size, cover the bowl tightly, and refrigerate it for 24 hours.

APPLES

Talk about comebacks. From an ominous intro-
duction in the Garden of Eden, apples have come full
circle to be celebrated as the fruit of choice. All areas of this
country have embraced apples as a delight second to none.
"As American as apple pie" is not just a cliché. The United
States is home to the world's largest apple growers, and hundreds of recipes are printed every fall offering creative uses for
the popular fruit. Our history is laced with apples, and in the
Southwest this is no exception. In the nineteenth century,
Native Americans and pioneers found lots of wild apples to
pick and enjoy. Apples were, and still are, abundant in northern New Mexico and Arizona. Inclusion of apples in just
about any Southwestern recipe is a natural combination.

Apples can be baked, boiled, or dried. They are so inher-
ently sweet, even tart varieties will leach enough moisture
and natural sugar to make a credible dish. Today, overspicing,
especially with cinnamon, is all too common. Flavor is de-
stroyed by overwhelming the natural tang of apple slices.

When selecting fresh apples, choose completely ripened,
mature apples. They should be smooth, have a rich color, and
be free of bruises or cuts. Refrigerate immediately. Unpeeled,
they will keep for at least a week. Wash well if using any part
of the skin. Peeled or unpeeled, dip in a mixture of ¼ cup
lemon juice to 1 quart water to prevent discoloration.

The following day, remove the dough and let it sit for an hour at room temperature. Form the dough into four 1-pound loaves of any shape you like. Try to get a tight seam under the loaves. Scatter cornmeal on baking trays, place the loaves on the tray, cover loaves with plastic wrap, and let them rise for approximately 4 to 6 hours. (Rising time will depend on the strength of the starter and the warmth of the room.)

Preheat oven to 375 degrees.

Use an oven stone if you have one. Bake loaves until dark golden brown (approximately 50 minutes). Spray water into your oven with a squirt bottle every five minutes for the first 20 minutes to create a nice steamy atmosphere for the crust, being sure not to spray the water directly onto the oven light or any heating elements.

YIELDS FOUR 1-POUND LOAVES

AUTHOR'S NOTE: If you don't have a white sourdough starter, you can do one of three things: (1) Ask a local sourdough baker if you can have some. Hopefully, the baker will encourage your experimentation; (2) Order some sourdough starter from a catalog, such as King Arthur Flour, 1-800-827-6836; (3) Make your own starter, which is great fun. There are many good baking books available that contain instructions for creating a sourdough starter.

~~~~~~~~~~~~~~

Jalapeño-Cheese-Tomato Baguette

Desert Flour Bakery and Bistro, Sedona, Arizona

BAKERS GARY WALD AND LILA STROTHER

6 ounces jalapeño peppers

3½ pounds (about 11 cups) bread flour

4 cups water

½ ounce fresh yeast

¼ cup honey

1 teaspoon salt

½ cup soft sun-dried tomatoes

4 ounces Cheddar cheese, diced into ½-inch cubes

Smoke the jalapeños in a smoker or on a grill. Dice and set aside.

In a large bowl, mix bread flour, water, yeast, and honey. If mixing by hand, use a wooden spoon until all is combined, about 10 minutes. If using an electric mixer, use a dough hook and mix until all is well combined, about 5 to 6 minutes.

Add salt. Mix 6 minutes.

Add peppers, tomatoes, and cheese. Knead 5 to 10 minutes. Let dough rest 1½ hours. Form into 2 loaves and place on well-greased oven-proof tray or cookie sheet. Cover and allow to rest until they have doubled in size, about 1 more hour.

Preheat oven to 425 degrees.

Bake for 35 minutes, misting occasionally with water.

YIELDS 2 LOAVES

AUTHOR'S NOTE: These loaves can be assembled without smoking the jalapeños, but they will lack an excellent flavoring.

~~~~~~~~~

Southwest Bread

Ilsa's Konditorei & Bakery,
Tucson, Arizona

BAKER ILSA BECHERT

3 cups warm water

1 ounce fresh yeast

¼ cup plus 2 tablespoons sugar

1½ ounces nonfat dry milk

¾ teaspoon salt

1 egg

8 to 10 cups unbleached flour

6½ tablespoons unsalted butter, melted

½ cup chopped black olives

½ cup chopped sun-dried tomatoes

1 tablespoon basil

In a large bowl, place warm water, yeast, sugar, dry milk, salt, and egg. Mix well. Add about half the flour. If mixing by hand, mix with a wooden spoon. If mixing with an electric mixer, use a dough hook to combine ingredients. When well blended, add butter and remaining flour. Add olives, tomatoes, and basil.

Knead dough for about 10 minutes until elastic, or knead until the dough bounces back when poked with your finger. Let the dough rise in a warm spot until it doubles in bulk. Punch down the dough and knead it lightly a few more times to get the remaining gas out. Divide the dough in half and form into 2 loaves. Place loaves on a well-greased cookie sheet or pizza pan and let them rise again until double in bulk.

Preheat oven to 325 degrees.

Slash the tops of the loaves gently with a very sharp knife or razor blade. Bake them for 30 to 35 minutes until they are brown and sound hollow when "thunked" with your fingers.

YEILDS 2 LOAVES

AUTHOR'S NOTE: This is a very attractive loaf, especially with a number of black olives exposed. If you do not want a round loaf, form and place in a well-greased loaf pan.

BELL PEPPERS

A BOUT A DECADE ago, most bell peppers came from the same plant. Now all varieties of bell pepper, including orange, purple, white, red, and yellow, come from hybrids dedicated to producing different fruits.

All bell peppers are members of the capsicum family, a large array of species with decidedly different characteristics. They are native to the western hemisphere, and pre-Inca tribes cultivated them thousands of years ago.

Although peak season for bell peppers is supposed to be August and September, you can usually find them year-round in supermarkets. Whatever the season, red bell peppers are always sweeter than green.

Bell peppers are an astounding source of vitamin C, actually containing more than citrus. They also contain a significant amount of vitamin A and a bit of calcium, phosphorus, iron, sodium, magnesium, thiamine, and niacin. The calorie count is the envy of the food kingdom: 22 calories for a green bell pepper and 31 for a ripened red one.

Bell peppers should be firm, shiny, nicely shaped, and rich in color, not pale. If wrapped or placed in a plastic storage bag, they should last in the refrigerator for up to seven days, but if cooked they last only one or two days.

To prepare, wash the entire pepper and cut off the top. Remove seeds and ribs. Use peppers whole, sliced, diced or chopped, raw or cooked, according to your recipe.

Honey Blue Cornmeal
Hearth Bread

BreadCrafters Bakery & Cafe,
Phoenix, Arizona

BAKER NANCY JOHNSON

6 to 6½ cups unbleached bread flour

2 cups blue cornmeal, plus extra for dusting baking sheets

1½ cups semolina flour

24 to 30 ounces cool water

¼ cup mesquite honey

2 tablespoons fresh yeast, packed

1 tablespoon salt

Nonstick vegetable oil spray

Parchment paper for lining two baking sheets

Raw pumpkin seeds for sprinkling on loaves (optional)

In a large, heavy work bowl, mix together 6 cups of the bread flour, blue cornmeal, and semolina flour. Stir well to combine.

Make a well in the center of the flour and add 2½ cups (20 ounces) of the water, the honey, and the yeast. Using your hands, mix the ingredients together. After the yeast has been mixed in well, add the salt. Add more water to make a coarse, sticky dough.

After the dough begins coming together, slam it onto the work surface several times, then cover it lightly with plastic wrap and let it rest for 10 minutes. After the rest, continue kneading the dough until it is smooth and pliable. (The dough should remain sticky as the cornmeal and semolina flour will absorb much of the moisture during fermentation.)

Clean your work bowl and spray it lightly with nonstick vegetable oil spray. Form the dough into a ball and place it in the work bowl. Spray the top of the dough with more nonstick vegetable oil spray and cover it lightly with plastic wrap.

Let the dough sit for 45 minutes and then punch it down and turn it over. Let it sit another 45 minutes until it is doubled in bulk.

Turn the dough out onto a work surface and divide it into four 1-pound pieces. Round each piece into a ball or mold it into fat oval loaves.

Line two baking sheets with parchment paper and dust the paper with blue cornmeal. Place 2 loaves onto each baking sheet and cover them lightly with a damp cloth or plastic wrap. Let the loaves rise for 45 minutes to 1 hour.

Thirty minutes before baking, preheat the oven to 450 degrees.

When the loaves have almost doubled in size and the dough springs back slightly when touched, uncover them, spray the tops with a fine mist of water, and sprinkle with pumpkin seeds. Slash each loaf once across the top with a sharp blade or razor.

Place the loaves in the oven, mist the oven with water (avoiding the oven light and heating elements), and quickly close the oven door. Immediately turn down the oven temperature to 400 degrees.

In 5 minutes, mist the oven with water again.

Let the loaves bake until deep brown and crusty, about 35 to 45 minutes. Rotate placement of the loaves once during baking.

This bread freezes well if wrapped tightly and frozen on the day it is baked.

VARIATIONS: During the final kneading, you may add chopped apricots, toasted sunflower seeds, toasted pecan or walnut pieces, or golden raisins.

YIELDS FOUR 1-POUND LOAVES

Three-Pepper Polenta Bread

Pangaea Bakery and Cafe,
Prescott, Arizona

BAKERS NICOLE MARSHALL,
BILL COPPERSMITH, AND DAVE DEUTSCH

FOR THE SPONGE

- 3 cups warm water
- 1 teaspoon honey
- 1 package dry yeast (not the fast-rising type)
- 3 cups unbleached organic white flour (all-purpose or bread type)
- ½ cup organic whole wheat flour

Add warm water to your mixing bowl. Add the honey and yeast. Stir and let mixture sit for 10 minutes until it begins to foam and bubble. With a wooden spoon, mix in the white flour and the ½ cup whole wheat flour. Stir until the sponge is well incorporated, about 100 strokes. The sponge will be wet and have the consistency of a thick milkshake. Let it sit for about 45 minutes.

FOR THE FINISH

- 3 Anaheim or New Mexico chiles, roasted
- 2 chipotle peppers, canned and packed in 1 tablespoon adobo sauce
- 1½ cups roasted red bell pepper
- 1 cup organic whole wheat flour
- 3 cups organic white flour, plus extra for working the dough
- 1¼ cups coarse polenta

2 tablespoons olive oil

2 tablespoons sea salt

Vegetable oil for oiling bowl and cooking pans

Remove and discard the skins of the roasted chiles and chop the chiles coarsely. Purée the chipotle peppers with the adobo sauce and add the liquid to the chopped chiles.

When the sponge is ready, add the cup of whole wheat flour and 3 cups of white flour, the polenta, olive oil, sea salt, and all of the cooled pepper mixture. Stir the dough until it forms a shaggy mass. Turn dough out onto a clean kneading surface. Knead until the dough feels smooth and soft, like an earlobe. You may need to add some extra flour to keep the dough from sticking to your kneading surface. Put the dough in a lightly oiled bowl and cover it with a wet towel or plastic wrap. Let the dough rest until it doubles, approximately 45 minutes. Punch the dough down and let it rise again until it doubles again, approximately 25 minutes. Divide the dough into 2 equal pieces. You will need two 9 x 5-inch bread pans or 1 large cookie sheet. Lightly oil the pans or sheet.

To shape the pan loaves, on a lightly floured surface roll the dough into an 8-inch square. Roll it into a tight cylinder, pinch the seams to seal the bottom and ends, and place it on the oiled pans.

To shape the loaves for the cookie sheet, form the dough into 2 tight balls and place them seam side down about 2 inches apart on the pan. Let them rest in a warm place until doubled in size, approximately 45 minutes.

Preheat oven to 400 degrees.

Bake for 40 minutes or until golden brown. Cool before slicing.

VARIATIONS: Add 1½ cups pepper jack cheese. Dust the pans and tops of loaves with cornmeal for a rustic look.

YIELDS TWO 9 X 5-INCH LOAVES.

Glossary

~~~~~~~~~~

Aïoli—Garlic-flavored mayonnaise, made the same way as fresh mayonnaise but with peeled cloves of garlic incorporated.

Anaheim Chile—Usually green, but red ones are also sold in larger markets. Closely related to the New Mexico chile. Anaheims are mild on the chile scale; most anyone can eat them. See "Chiles," pages 4–9.

Ancho Chile—Dried poblano. Sometimes mistaken for the pasilla, another popular dried chile. See "Chiles," pages 4–9.

Arugula—A leafy vegetable with a spicy hot flavor. Only a few sprigs are necessary to enhance a dish.

Asadero Cheese—A soft white cheese much like jack but with more flavor. Made with skim milk.

Asiago Cheese—Originally a goat's milk cheese, it is now primarily made with cow's milk. Very flavorful hard cheese, sometimes called a poor man's Parmesan. Imported from Italy or domestically made.

Azafrán—A Native American saffron. Although not in the same plant family, azafrán and saffron taste very similar. If substituting, one pinch of saffron equals two tablespoons of azafrán.

Balsamic Vinegar—Made from Trebbiano grapes. Found in many specialty stores, it is well aged, dark, sweet, and pungent. There is no substitute. See "Vinegar," page 71.

Beans—Hundreds of varieties of pod-producing plants. See "Beans," pages 30–31, and the specific bean types that follow.

Anasazi—Long used by Native Americans, relatively new on grocery shelves. Spotted reddish-brown and white and medium in size. Pintos can be substituted in a pinch.

Black—Thought to be native to South America but used in many Southwestern recipes. Deep black color.

Garbanzo—Also called "chickpea." Round and tan-colored, they are readily available dried or canned. Popular in salads and stews or mashed to make hummus.

Butternut Squash—Popular winter squash, gourd-shaped and fully tan in color when ripe.

Cayenne Pepper—One of the most popular chiles in powder form. Valuable in many sauces and soups. Easily obtained at most grocery stores. See "Chiles," pages 4–9.

Chayote Squash—Elongated in shape, a winter squash that is usually green but is also white in some regions. Lots of ridges and grooves form a rough exterior.

Chipotle Pepper—A dried and smoked jalapeño. In the middle range in terms of heat. It tastes smoky and sweet. See "Chiles," pages 4–9.

Cilantro—This herb, thought to be Spanish in origin, is found worldwide in bunches much like parsley but with a much stronger flavor. Leaves are usually removed from stems for use. Also called "Chinese parsley" or "coriander" in its fresh, leafy form.

Coriander—Usually found in stores as a powder or a small seed that is only about ⅛ inch in diameter. Very popular around the world and readily available. Tastes like a combination of cumin and caraway.

Coulis—Also simply called "sauce."

Deglazing—The technique of creating a thick liquid to add intense flavoring to a dish. The process is easier than it sounds. To deglaze, remove cooked items from the cooking pan, leaving only liquid. Add the suggested liquid, such as wine, and bring to a boil while stirring frequently and scraping loose any food bits stuck to the bottom of the pan. Reduce the mixture to a thin syrup. If you reduce it too much, simply add a few additional tablespoons of liquid and reduce again.

Eggplant—Treated as a vegetable, though it is really a large, pear-shaped fruit, deep purple in color. Very mild flavor. See "Eggplant," page 47.

Elephant Garlic—Large bulb of garlic, about the size of a chicken egg. Use as you would any garlic.

Fennel Bulb—A vegetable with a thick stalk and bulb base, found in many produce sections. May be eaten raw, but is usually combined with other ingredients. Tasty substitute for celery. See "Fennel," page 21.

Fennel Seeds—Yellow-brown in color with a hint of licorice flavor.

Feta Cheese—A natural goat's milk cheese.

Flautas—Taking their name from the Spanish for "flute," these tightly filled corn tortillas are assembled, rolled, and usually fried before serving.

Gazpacho—Spanish in origin. A soup of fresh vegetables, found in many forms and allowing for very creative mixtures. There are no right or wrong ingredients.

Hatch Chili—A sweet, mild chile from Mexico. Anaheims may be substituted.

Hominy—A dried corn product made by removing the germ. Will puff up when properly cooked. Also found in flaked form called "grits." See "Hominy," page 140.

Jalapeño Jack Cheese—Jalapeño-flavored cheese, usually mixed with jack or Monterey jack. Spicy.

Jalapeño Pepper—Very popular chile available in stores in most regions of the United States. Mild to hot in flavor. See "Chiles," pages 4–9.

Jicama—A brown root that looks much like a turnip. Tastes very similar to water chestnuts but is sweeter.

Kosher Salt—Kosher salt is more coarsely grained than table salt and is only about half as salty in flavor. Substitute table salt, but use less.

Leek—Related to onions but with a much milder flavor. Found in long stalks. Usually only the white portion is used.

Lemon Grass—A strawlike stalk with a lemony flavor. Found most often in Asian markets.

Lentils—There are several kinds, the most popular being brown lentils. Excellent vegetarian replacement for minced meat in most recipes. One of the few beans that can be cooked without soaking.

Masa Harina—A basic corn flour mixture specially prepared for making tortillas. If unavailable, use a standard tortilla masa recipe (found in many Mexican cookbooks).

Miso Paste—A fermented soybean product, usually found in the cheese section of major grocery markets or natural food stores.

Mole—Originally from the Nahuatl Indian word *molli,* meaning a sauce made with chile peppers. Now generally thought to be a Spanish-Mexican spicy sauce, usually made with an unsweetened chocolate. Can be both. See "Mole," page 54.

Morel—Cone-shaped brown mushroom with a meaty texture. Should be easy to find. Wonderful flavor, but more common button mushrooms will substitute. See "Mushrooms," page 136.

Nixtamal—A treated, dried corn mixture and direct substitute for dried hominy. When fully processed it is called masa and is usually used to make tortillas. See "Hominy," page 140.

Nopales—Pads of prickly pear cactus, picked when young and green. See "Prickly Pear," page 108.

Nopalito—Pickled prickly pear cactus pads.

Orzo—A small shaped pasta, also called "barley pasta." Looks more like rice than pasta.

Paella—A Spanish casserole usually containing saffron and just about anything else on the kitchen shelf. Varieties are endless.

Pappardelle—A broad, flat, egg noodle.

Penne—Pasta tubes cut diagonally at both ends into short lengths. Also called "mostaccioli."

Pepitas—Mexican-style pumpkin seeds, medium dark green in color and larger than those grown in the United States. Available raw or roasted, hulled or unhulled. They are sold in most natural food and many grocery stores, as well as by mail order.

Phyllo Dough—Thin pastry sheets. Making your own is a challenge. Best to buy prepared, then thaw and peel sheets according to package instructions.

Pine Nuts/Piñons—A popular Southwestern nut that tastes a little like an almond. Used by Native Americans in many dishes, including ground as a flour for breadlike products. Buy shelled since it is very difficult to extract the meat.

Polenta—A thick meal usually made from cornmeal.

Portabello Mushroom—Deep, rich flavor, brown in color. Large and looks like a thatched roof. Wonderful blended into a recipe or simply grilled. Purchase fresh. See "Mushrooms," page 136.

Potato

> **Red**—Usually thought of as a "new potato." Red skin with a crisp, white flesh. Many varieties are sold, but rarely identified by any other name than "red potato." As a new potato, it is smaller and typically lower in starch.

> **Russet**—The most popular of all American potatoes, usually baked unpeeled. Dark brown in color. Has the highest starch content of all potatoes.

> **Yukon Gold**—Relatively new on the market. A soft, creamy and tasty potato. Slightly gold in color and looks like it has already been buttered. Delicious.

Quinoa—A fruit native to the high Andes and now found in many natural food stores. Used like a grain. Sweet flavor and soft texture. Pale in color when purchased fresh. Served much like rice.

Ragout—Cut, cooked, and well-seasoned vegetables (and/or meat), combined in a rich sauce. From the French, meaning "stew."

Ratatouille—A stew of French origin with eggplant and squash.

Red Pepper—Another name for the common red bell pepper. See "Bell Peppers," page 153.

Red Rice—A Wehani or Basmati hybrid rice grown in California. Turns a deep russet color when cooked. It has a unique, complex flavor, but white rice will do if unavailable.

Red Swiss Chard—Looks similar to spinach but has thicker stems. Tastes stronger. Wash well—it is usually sandy. Can be shredded for salads or cooked. Central stem is particularly good when cut into lengths and steamed.

Roux—A common flour-based thickening agent. See "Making a Roux," page 25.
Sabayon—"Sauce."

Semolina—This flour milled of durum wheat is the commonly used flour in pastas. Most recipes will allow substitution with unbleached flour.

Serrano Chile—A hot chile used in sauces or as an accent. See "Chiles," pages 4–9.

Shiitake Mushroom—Chinese and Japanese fungi, best when young. Can be used in a number of dishes. Found dried and fresh. To reconstitute dried shiitakes, soak in hot water for 30 minutes and drain. Soaking in water makes an excellent vegetable stock. See "Mushrooms," page 136.

Terrine—Originally an earthenware dish soaked in water before use in cooking. Term has expanded to include almost any dish made in such a pot.

Tofu—A compressed soybean-milk curd high in protein, vitamins and minerals. Usually found chilled in small plastic boxes in produce sections. See "Tofu," page 43.

Tomatillo—Small, slightly tart yellow or green tomatoes, usually found wrapped in a thin husk. Discard the husk before use. Tomatillos tend to stay firm when cooked.

Tomato—See "Tomatoes," pages 80–81, and the specific types that follow.

    Beefsteak—Popular homegrown variety, very large, firm, and delicious in salads.

    Plum—Also called "Italian plum." Contains a large amount of liquid, so it is a popular ingredient in sauces.

    Roma Thick walls, small seeds, great for cooking. Very similar to plum tomatoes in texture and taste.

Tortilla—A flat, thin, unleavened bread used to wrap various ingredients. Can be corn or flour based. Found in packages at most markets.

Tatsoi—Baby bok choy, sometimes called "Chinese cabbage." Used in many stir-fry dishes.

Vegetable Stock—A cooking liquid easily made by cooking leftover vegetables in a large pot of water, then straining out vegetables and keeping liquid. See "Vegetable Stocks," pages 124–25.

Wonton Skin—Used as a wrap, much like a tortilla, but smaller. Found prepackaged (usually one pound) in most Asian markets. Varies in shape from round to square. Easy to use, difficult to make yourself.

Index

Grilled Vegetable Salad, 69–70
Santa Fe Vegetarian Harvest Platter
    with Grilled Vegetables, Heirloom
    Beans, Roasted Tomato Salsa, and
    Tree Fruit Tamales, 77–79
Groban, Reed, 41
Gross, Christopher J., 126–127
Güero chiles. *See* Yellow hot wax chiles

Habanero chiles, 8, *8*
Hartnett, Margaret, 56–58
The Heartline Café, 15, 63–64
Heenan, Rick, 146–147
High Desert Inn, 56–58
Hill, Jon, 73
Hominy, 140
Honey Blue Cornmeal Hearth Bread,
    154–155
Hornos, 76

Ilsa's Konditorei & Bakery, 151 152
Inn of the Anasazi, 45–46

Jalapeño chiles, 8, *8*
Jalapeño-Chayote Slaw, *110,* 113
Jalapeño Cheese Bread, 146–147
Jalapeño-Cheese-Tomato Baguette,
    150–151
Red Chile and Jalapeño Fettucine with
    Cilantro Cream and Toasted
    Walnuts, 122–123
Janos, 70 72
Johnson, Nancy, 154–155

Kagel, Katharine, 119–120
Kamnitzer, Erasom "Razz," 22–23, 88–89
Kaufman, Chrysa, 138–139
Kidney beans, *31*
Kowalske, Robert, 97–99
Kramer, Albert, 137

La Casa Sena Restaurant and Cantina,
    26, 77–79
Las Ventanas, 41
Lash, Matthew, 75
Leithe, Jan K., 28–*29*
Lemon-Garlic Aïoli, 64
Lentils, *31*
Lentil Cakes, 138–139
Lentil Cakes with Nopalito and
    Arizona Apples Relish, 88–89
Lima beans, *31*
Lime-Cilantro Crema, 38
Luethje, Chad, 14

Maguire, Kevin E., 59–60
Manzanita Restaurant, 137
Maple
Cinnamon Maple Cream, 17–19, *18*
Marshall, Nicole, 156–157
Matney, Eddie, 19–20, 133–135
Mesquite-Roasted Yellow Tomato Soup
    with Piñon-Cilantro Pesto and Crispy
    Potato Curls, 45–46
Michael's at the Citadel, 32–34, 129–131
Mole, 54
Polenta and Pine Nut-Stuffed Red
    Peppers with Mole, 56–58, *57*
Pumpkin Seed Mole, *100,* 103–104
Vegetables in Mole Verde, 53–55
Morels
Chipotle Crema Morel Stew in Acorn
    Squash, 119–120, *121*
Muffins
Chocolate-Raspberry Muffins, *143,*
    145–146
Pepper-Corn Muffins, *57, 143,* 144–145
Murphy's Restaurant, 69–70
Mushrooms, 136
Grilled Portabello Mushrooms with
    Southwestern Black Beans, Corn
    Relish, and Goat Cheese, *132,*
    133–135
Roasted Garlic, Mushroom, and Broccoli
    Dumplings in Gingered Broth,
    32–35, *33*
Wild Mushroom Ragout with Green
    Chile-Spiked Polenta, 82–83
Native American cuisine, 76
Nellies, 114–115
New Mexican chiles, 4, 8, *8*
New Mexican Harvest Vegetables in Crisp
    Phyllo with Peach-Chile Coulis and
    Jalapeño-Chayote Slaw, *110,* 111–113
Nopales
Nopalito Cactus and Arizona Apples
    Relish, 89
Polenta with Summer Vegetables and
    Roasted Nopales, 105–107
Norby, Amy, 37–38
Northern beans, *31*

The Oaks Restaurant, 66–67
Oils
Basil oil, 72
Sun-Dried Tomato Oil, 72
Olives
Poblano Chiles Stuffed with Pasta,
    Olives, and Sun-Dried Tomatoes, 75

About the Author

L on Walters says he never had to be forced to clean his plate at dinner time, and that cooking and baking have always been a serious hobby. Upon retiring from a twenty-one-year Naval Aviation career, he opened a large bakery in San Diego.

For the last five years, Lon has written a weekly food column for the *Sedona Red Rock News,* and he and his wife, Margi, operate as a successful real estate sales team in Sedona. Lon and Margi enjoy cooking and baking, horseback riding, and vintage car events. They also enjoy caring for a lengthy list of pets, including horses, dogs, cats, birds, and a turtle.

Lon's first cookbook, *The Old West Baking Book,* also from Northland Publishing, is a historical treatment of baking in the Southwest in the nineteenth century, a project that gave him a great appreciation for indigenous ingredients in recipes. This book is a continuation of his love of the Southwest and of the wonderfully complex cuisine of the area.